FROM
FOSTER
CARE

WITH A
Purpose

NATASHA JORDAN

FROM FOSTER CARE WITH A *Purpose*

Cover art by: Professional Identity Partners

Editing & formatting by:
RIA JAY Publishing www.riajay.com
Shawneya Ellis Publishing www.shawneyaellis.com
The Creating Change Publishing www.creatingchange.com

ISBN 979-8-9887614-0-2 (Paperback)
Printed in the United States of America
First printing August 2023

For additional copies, email us at:
Publishing@AllThingsNatashaJ.com
www.allthingsnatashaj.com

Dedication

To My Mother and Foster Mother

Words cannot express how much you both mean to me. Thank you ladies, for raising me especially, during the times that I was difficult. May you both continue to rest in peace.

To my amazing readers

It is my hope that whether you need guidance or seeking to navigate through a circumstance in life, my story will inspire, grow, and strengthen you!

Acknowledgment

I would like to acknowledge everyone who supported my journey of writing, *From Foster Care with a Purpose*. Your belief, constant support, and trust in me, helped to birth this labor of love. Thank you for the dedication of those who reviewed every aspect of the book. It is because of you that I can encourage those who will read, *From Foster Care with a Purpose*. My heart truly belongs to you. Thank you!

CONTENTS

Preface …………………………………………12

Chapter 1   Mom and I   …………………………...14

Chapter 2   New York, New York   …………………25

Chapter 3   All Under One Roof ……………………45

Chapter 4   Chaos brings Change ………………......53

Chapter 5   A Ward of the Court – Part One…….......58

A Ward of the Court - Part Two………..83

Chapter 6   Home Sweet Foster Home …………..….90

Chapter 7   A New Family …………………………103

Chapter 8   Fostering Relationships ………………..116

Chapter 9   An Entrepreneur Was Born……………125

Chapter 10 A Child's Action Plan …………………144

Conclusion ……………………………………155

About the Author

Natasha Jordan was born to a mother whom she loved and cared for no matter the circumstances. She was raised as a foster child by an amazing foster mother who taught her that her situation did not define her. Values such as hard work and never giving up was instilled in Ms. Jordan at an early age. Through this book, the author will share life-changing experiences, as well as offer individuals the tools to move their lives in a positive direction.

From Foster Care with a Purpose, is one of many writings to come. Natasha aims to provide inspiration, motivation, and information to empower others. It is her hope that her story will birth independence and encourage others to sustain mental and spiritual wellness.

Preface

Some may wonder how an average girl from North Carolina who was born into a loving family ended up in foster care. Just the same, some may view the foster care system as a harsh reality. However, I'm here to tell you that it's not as black and white as you may think. No doubt there are foster care horror stories, but my foster care experience was quite different. Initially, I was just your average girl, who grew up in your average neighborhood, until life was not so average, anymore. I soon learned the harsh reality of what life was all about. At the time, I was too young to understand the complexities of my actions. My words and my decisions created a domino effect that ended up out of my control and landed me in the system. As a child I did not understand; as an adult I came to realize the decisions and the difficulties that I encountered shaped my view and purpose in life.

Yes, while I did become a child who was eventually raised by the foster care system, I thank God that I was placed somewhere that showed me how great life was capable of being. As I look back, I have no one to thank other than the people who raised me. I am not saying that my foster care experience was perfect; it was far from it. However, through it all the love of my foster mother was exactly what I needed, genuinely received, and appreciated.

As I look back, now I realize that my life experiences in foster care was only to help me reach back and help others who are navigating the same journey. So, while some may view the foster care experience as unfortunate, I feel that it shaped me to be the person I am today. Sometimes God uses certain individuals as vessels to reach the masses, and I now know that He gifted me with the purpose of helping others. As I work to change the lives of individuals who share a similar fate, I will never lose sight of where I came from. I can attest that my daily journey is dedicated to loving, listening, and leading with purpose. Through my story, I hope to help other's walk towards change and success.

CHAPTER 1

MOM & I

Parenting is one of the toughest jobs that anyone can ever have. It's not your traditional 9-5 job. No. Parenting is a lifetime commitment and sometimes, it can get challenging, especially for single parents. So, I am sure that you can imagine some of the difficulties my mother faced as a single, teenage mom in the seventies. Not only that, but her battle with bipolar disorder and paranoid schizophrenia created a separate host of issues.

My mother was only fourteen years old when she gave birth to me. Although she was young and still learning life, she loved me from the moment she laid eyes on me. As my tiny body laid on her chest, an instant mother and daughter bond was formed. Although she couldn't always contribute monetarily, we were blessed with a strong support system. My grandmother, grandfather, and aunt surrounded us with love and provided as much assistance as we needed.

Though my mother strived to be a good parent, she was still a child herself and longed to live her teenage life. Feeling confined under my grandmother's strict rules, she made it her primary mission to find a way to get out of the house. Like many teenagers, she was very feisty and took pleasure in going out partying and hanging out with her friends. This left my grandmother with the responsibility of raising me. My mother gave birth to me, but it was my grandmother that cared for me daily. My grandmother treated me like I was her own child, and in a sense, I was. Afterall, she was raising my mother and myself simultaneously. Looking back, I am thankful for the guidance that she provided to me, and my mother.

My mom may have appeared to have it easy with my grandmother looking after me, but life wasn't as sweet as it may have seemed. At an early age, she experienced troubles that would change her life forever. She lost her innocence at the hand of people entrusted to protect and care for her. Being molested by a family member can leave a permanent scar on your life, and when others don't believe in your truth, it can lead you down a dark road. This trauma only added to her on-going mental health issues; she became fearful of certain family members and started experiencing a period of mental distress.

I know by now you're wondering where my father was during all of this. Well, just like my mom he was just a young kid. He was lost in the streets with struggles of his own. He was raised by women and had no male role models to guide him. The streets were all he knew. So how could this young man with no guidance or help raise a little baby? Don't get me wrong, my father wasn't a bad kid, just misguided, often using the streets to meet his needs. Though I didn't see him often, that didn't stop the love that I had for him and being the fact that I was his first born, I was in awe of him. Even though he was an absentee father, he brightened up my day the 1-2 times a year that he did come around. However, he did give me one of the greatest gifts I have in my life, my baby sister. While our relationship is not without challenges; we have grown extremely close over the years, and I love her unconditionally.

Sometimes, I wondered if his presence would have made an impact on my life, but I also know it's unhealthy to live in the past. Often, we rack our brains with questions that we will never know the answer to, but to be honest, I think my destiny would have still turned out the same. I felt that my dad was just too young to be a father. Even though my mother was young as well, she was more mature and had guidance in her life.

Sometimes wherever we go, monsters continue to trail us like extremely dark shadows. However, according to my mother, she gained a little strength the moment I was born. She knew she would not be alone in this world, but somehow, she failed to realize how unbelievably cruel the world would be to her.

I saw my mother through various stages of her life, especially when she left me alone with grandma. I still knew in my heart of hearts how much she loved me. The first time I recall my mother's mental illness; being an issue was when I was five. It was then I noticed a shift in the atmosphere at home. My mother began binge partying, and it spiraled out of control. She would often be out for days, leaving me at my grandmother and aunt's mercy.

There is one time that stands out in my mind—this was when she did not return home. Though my mother was known for her careless behavior, this time was different. The house phone rang, and the news that my grandmother received from the other line was chilling. My mom was found wandering and hallucinating in a neighboring town after partying with a few of her friends. This episode had become so bad that my uncle had to pick her up and my grandmother had to admit her to a state-run psychiatric hospital.

My young mind couldn't comprehend what was happening at the time. It appeared as if everything was chaotic, and nothing was no longer normal. Experiencing the vestiges of our household slip from my grasp was overwhelming and extremely difficult to process. Imagine a young girl already missing the presence of her mother, and then being stripped away from her for a prolonged period. I remember visiting mom at the hospital and being terrified of that place. I can only imagine how scared and alone she felt while she was in there.

As I walked up to the imposing brown building, holding my grandmother's hand tightly, I passed by people wearing crisp white uniforms. The entire building was white on the inside, with the smell of antiseptic hanging thickly in the air. All the nurses and doctors wore white caps and lab coats resembling bright specters of doom. They seemed eerily unapproachable, and I was terrified by them. They all walked around with stern expressions as they cared for their patients. Looking back, there seemed to be no softness to their approach.

The facility was so sterile that you literally could not see a speck of dust if it landed on the furniture. Seeing my mother there was devastating; it instantly broke my heart. Confused, I struggled to understand what was happening and often questioned what was wrong with her. Even though I was young, and I didn't have any life experience yet, this wasn't normal, and she didn't deserve the ordeal she was being subjected to. I wanted to hug her so badly to make her feel safe the way she made me feel. But I was too young to know what it would take to console her.

The sheer lack of proper treatment caused her to get worse before getting better. After all it was the seventies the medical and psychiatric personnel didn't have the knowledge, expertise, and resources that they have at their disposal today. In today's time, we have more qualified and experienced medical and psychiatric professionals, social workers, caseworkers, and therapists. In addition, the institutions were often overcrowded, understaffed, and staffed with unqualified personnel. As a result of these obstacles many patients were confined to their rooms for long periods of time, restrained or secluded to padded rooms as a form of punishment. Quite frankly a significant lack of privacy and personal autonomy for patients did not exist. Patients were often stripped of their personal belongings, including clothing, and were required to wear hospital gowns. They were also subjected to invasive procedures, which were sometimes used as a form of punishment rather than a legitimate treatment. In addition, there was a significant stigma surrounding mental illness during this time, which often led to patients being mistreated or overlooked by healthcare professionals and society at large.

Sometimes when I would visit my mother, I would find her crying, terrified at the thought of where she was. I couldn't blame her, the facility looked more like a tortuous white prison than a rehabilitation center created to help patients. You could see the fear in some of the patients' eyes, others were so highly medicated they walked around like zombies. Most times, my mother would be so heavily sedated that her eyes would roll into the back of her head. Could you imagine what it was like as a young child witnessing your mother transforming into a person that you barely knew? I remember thinking that a monster was overtaking her body and inflicting extreme pain unto her. Now, when I think about it, in a way, I was right.

It was hard to watch my mom in this condition. Even as a child, I knew I had to comfort her. I was her light in a world of darkness. Sometimes when I visited her, I would hug her and rub her head, imitating how she would calm me whenever I would start crying. She would become calmer whenever I did that. It wasn't easy to watch my mother confined in that terrible hospital. It felt like I was losing her, and I was the only connection she had to her lost soul. My mother didn't stay there long. Once she was free, I would watch as she encountered the cycle of having mental breakdowns over the years.

Though my mother and grandmother loved each other, they never had a great bond. However, this did not stop my grandmother for caring for her daughter. It was she who played doctor; sitting guard so that my mother would not leave the house, giving her the medications that she needed, feeding her, and being attentive. I would watch how my grandma would nurse my mother back to health. This was a heavy burden on my grandmother, however, she did all she could to care for her only daughter. But even with all the support and supervision my grandmother provided, there were times where mom's condition would worsen. Out of options, this was when grandmother would have her hospitalized.

My mom did her best to raise me with the help of my grandparents, aunt, and two favorite cousins. She bought me the best clothes, and my grandma and aunt provided the food, shelter, and housing; my cousins stepped in and nurtured me. Everyone contributed to giving me a stable life. But soon, my mother felt that being a southern girl was boring. She thought the best way to live up to her potential was to move to New York with other family members. That's when I was left to be raised by my grandmother, aunt, and cousins full-time. This time, however, it was more a matter of choice than circumstance. That's why when my mother announced her decision to move, my grandma worried a lot about it. Yet, she continued to stand by her daughter. She did that only to see her happy.

We had an uncle that lived in New York. He decided to help Mom move, and before I knew it, my mom had left. I felt alone, even with a house full of people; I thought mom was leaving *me*. Back then, I didn't understand much about her condition and the importance of her having to move. Like any child feels when a parent leaves them, I thought it was my fault my mother had to go. It was only later that I realized how much she still loved me with all her heart. Memories flooded my mind with special mother/daughter times we shared. I lived for those moments and could tell that mom did too. Though we talked on the phone often and she came back a few times a year to visit, it was different from being in the presence of each other daily. Not long after moving, she began to miss me unbearably, just as I missed her. As great as life was with my grandma and aunt, they weren't my mom. I needed her in my life

just as much as she needed me.

CHAPTER 2

NEW YORK, NEW YORK

I spent nearly the first decade of my life with my grandparents. They were my saving grace and an extremely impactful part of my life. My grandmother was tall, with beautiful, long jet-black hair. Her melanated skin was dark and smooth. She had a relaxed demeanor, but her presence and voice commanded attention when she walked in a room. Most people thought that grandma was mean, but she was my best friend, and the most loving and caring person I knew. Throughout my childhood, she always had health issues, but she pressed on despite her physical health.

My grandfather, on the other hand, was quite the opposite. He was a quiet, short, and stocky man, who allowed my grandmother to lead the family. He worked hard to provide for his family, he was an awesome grandfather. I am most appreciative of the way he took care of us even though he was not my mom's biological father. His presence in my life definitely made him my first male role model.

I was nine when I realized how much I missed my mother. Life seemed boring without her. The dysfunction seemed like excitement at my age. I couldn't set aside the emptiness that crept within every day that passed without my mother's presence. My grandma knew how much we missed seeing each other, so once I mustered up the courage to ask if I could visit New York for the summer, she obliged.

Though my grandmother was stern, I would grow to miss her gentle, yet corrective guidance just as I would miss my grandfather's meek nature. However, even though I knew that I would miss them, thoughts of being with my mom flooded my mind and gave me hope. I was able to find happiness and contentment because I was finally going to have the missing piece of my life…my mother.

I remember it like it was yesterday. It was a Saturday morning when I left for New York. At this time, I was oblivious to how visiting my mother would become a turning point in my life and how it would shape my future. Would I have still asked to go if

I knew how much my life would change? I don't know for certain, but what I do know is after I left North Carolina, my life would never be the same. My grandmother and grandfather had tears in their eyes as they drove to the airport. They were reluctant to let me visit New York— little did we know, I would not return home.

Once we arrived at the airport, we completed the check-in process. During the 80's parents and guardians were allowed to accompany minors to the departure gate, so we proceeded to the security check point together. After clearing security, we sat at the departure gate until it was time for me to get on the plane. My grandparents and I were soon greeted by a flight attendant. She was a nice lady with a gentle voice, and pretty hair. She informed us that she would be escorting me onto the flight and caring for me while onboard. Oddly, she brought a feeling of security, though she was a complete stranger.

"Are you ready, honey?" She asked with a smile on her face.

I nodded yes.

That was a cue to my grandmother and grandfather who stood up, said they loved me and gave me a hug. I took her hand;

turning back to wave goodbye to the only family I knew; who had given me so much love. I ran back, gave my grandparents another hug, and began walking down the tunnel to board the large aircraft. It was my first plane ride. I suppose many children would be fearful, but I was perfectly comfortable. As I think back, it's amazing as a child how brave I was on my first plan ride; now as an adult, I am scared once the plane takes off.

My brown eyes widened with excitement as I stared out the window. The higher the plane climbed into the sky, the smaller the buildings became; eventually disappearing and being replaced by the clouds. It all felt like magic. I had eaten a few snacks, talked with the lady sitting next to me, fallen asleep, and woken up at my destination. I opened my eyes to the flight attendant softly telling me it was time to go. Boy, oh boy! Was my adrenaline rushing? I was going to see my mother again. And this time, I would make sure we spent the most time together. The flight attendant and I walked hand in hand down another tunnel, and I joyfully hopped and skipped toward the end of it.

There were so many people there, new faces, and they all looked so different and happy. But even in the huge crowd, my eyes immediately fell on this petite lady with a radiant smile that revealed the slight gap in her teeth. Her short hairstyle showed off her beautiful face and she was dressed so stylishly. It was my mom. As soon as I saw her, I let go of the flight attendant's hand and ran up to her, hopping into her eager, waiting arms. Mom laughed as she hugged me tight, tears of joy filling her eyes.

"I missed you, baby," she whispered, and I smiled as I hugged her tighter. Her embrace made me feel so safe. I never wanted to let go, and the way she was holding me, it was clear she didn't want too either. We walked to the baggage claim smiling at each other. She was so beautiful, and I gleamed at her with admiration. I am sure people noticed how happy both of us were. My pink butterfly suitcase wasn't too difficult to spot, and mom grabbed it as we walked to a car waiting outside.

Everything looked so different than back home. People were bustling about, and there was a high level of excitement in the atmosphere. My little mind was infected by the positive and warm energy that fumed the air. The most noticeable sound I remember is the honking of the impatient cars. People really couldn't wait to be off and on their way. I looked around in awe and got into the waiting car with my mom. An unfamiliar man sat in the driver's seat and greeted us with a smile. Their energy matched one another, complementing each other well. Upon entering the car, she took his hand.

"Sweetie, say hello to my boyfriend," she said.

"Hi," I beamed. He replied with just as much enthusiasm, and I immediately thought I liked him. As we drove off, I looked around at the city. It was so different from back home. There were tall buildings, big building, and a lot of people hustling and bustling, throughout the city I couldn't get enough of it all. Then mom said something that immediately grabbed my attention.

"Are you hungry?" She said, glancing at the backseat where I sat entranced, watching the many fascinating landmarks as we passed them by.

"Yes!" I replied, a little too happily. It made both my mom and her boyfriend chuckle.

"Well, would you like to have McDonald's?" Mom stated. I squealed, "Mom, how did you know?!"

Mom laughed. Her eyes gleaming with happiness.

"I am your mom, of course, I know!" she replied with a big smile.

I felt like we were a little old family; I was glad that mom's boyfriend was a great guy. When I got to my mom's apartment, I was even more shocked to see the tall building she lived in. I still remember how I told her I thought it was a hotel. She laughed as she tousled my hair, telling me it wasn't. I couldn't understand it then, but as I grew up I realized that all that glitters isn't gold. As a kid, everything seemed exciting and new. As the years passed, I realized that there was nothing glamourous about that tall building. It was merely government owned housing for low-income families, better known as 'the projects.'

I didn't settle in right away; it took me a while to get accustomed to my new surroundings. I was a curious child and quite sociable, so it was fun meeting the new kids. Unfortunately, not every child I met was welcoming, nor friendly. In fact, a few of them were the neighborhood bullies.

The more time I spent in New York, the more I realized how much I missed my grandmother and the rest of the family. Even though mom was mentally stable, and things were going well, as the weeks went by, I became homesick. It wasn't easy for a nine-year-old to leave behind the only family she knew. I asked my mom when I could go back home to grandma and that's when I got the shock of my life.

Mom told me that I would not be going back . That's when I realized this trip was not just a visit—it was permanent. I instantly became numb. I could feel the tears swell my eyes. I was distraught because no matter how great my life seemed at the moment with my mom; all I ever knew was my grandma and my life back home. She was my safety blanket, and my protector when mom was not well. It was a lot for me to process. With the knowledge I had now, the fairytale I had walked into suddenly changed. It was as if I knew, at that moment, that my life was going to transform. And it did, but it wasn't for the better.

Living life with mom was not that bad, at least not at first. Mom's boyfriend was very nice. I had never met any of her boyfriends before, so I didn't know what to expect. However, I would say that it was refreshing to see how much he cared. He was always making sure we were okay, and the more time we spent together, the more comfortable I became in his presence. The only bad part about him was that he was a heavy drinker and when he was drunk, he and my mom would get into physical fights.

The first time I saw them fight, everything I knew about relationships changed. Before this, I had never seen a man raise their hand to strike a woman. The women in my family were too strong for that. That's why watching the fight between mom and her boyfriend was something completely new and horrifying for me. Mom and her boyfriend fought every Friday when he got paid. It was the same thing, every week, like clockwork. He would give her money and then go across the street with his friends to get drunk.

When he was sufficiently drunk, he would come home, and mom was not interested in anything that he would say. The cycle would then repeat itself. He would throw a punch, and mom would throw another, and finally, exhausted by the physical exertion, they would go to sleep. That summed up our weekend. It is not the best memory I have, but even if I wanted to, I cannot erase it. It is something that is still engraved in my mind.

Their physical fights weren't the only traumatizing thing I had to endure. Due to my mom's illness, she often accused me of being disrespectful. I think the pressures of raising me on her own and without the support of immediate family brought about a new wave of stress, and with stress came a spike in her mental illnesses. Mom came from an era of "yes ma'am" and "no ma'am." An era where children were to be seen, not heard and where adults were always right. So, if I did or said anything that she felt challenged her; she would lash out at me. Many times, she would think I had done something wrong when I hadn't done anything at all. Her mental illness caused her to utilize extreme discipline that led to me getting beaten regularly. I do feel spankings are acceptable, however

I oppose children being physically and verbally abused — that's not discipline.

Though discipline is needed, it shouldn't be done out of anger or to instill fear. Mom's way of disciplining me physically hurt me. At one point, I was terrified of her. What child wouldn't be terrified of someone who hits them? Despite everything, she was still my mother, and nothing would stop me from loving her the way I did. The beatings got worse whenever my mother had a mental breakdown. I did not always understand why she would beat me so often; but I accepted it. I was too young to resist, nowhere to hide in our apartment, and I had no one to protect me. I quickly learn that her own upbringing and her mental illness controlled her mind and moods. I would always second-guess myself and look over my shoulder. I would often think that I was not a good enough child or that had done something wrong to upset her. Mom would beat me with anything she found nearby – belts, tree limbs, and extension cords. It scared me to be around her on some occasions and yet, I still wanted the love of my mother.

Mom's mental breakdowns were scary, and nerve wracking to me. I didn't know what to expect from her when the episodes occurred; even though I knew what to expect. There was one weekend mom had a mental breakdown, the first one in a long time. That weekend, she was not herself. She began to talk in a language that I did not understand, but it was familiar behavior. Right away, thoughts of my grandma flooded my mind, and I began to fervently hope that she would magically appear in front of me to help me out of the situation. Of course, that never happened.

Mom was yelling about the house not being clean, and her OCD behavior began to kick in. She was a perfectionist when it came to cleaning, which is perhaps why she worked as a housekeeper at a local hospital. I helped her that day as she cleaned obsessively. Later, we had brunch, and Mom went off to bed. I did not disturb her while she was sleeping; she looked so at peace. That day, she slept until it was time for her to go to work that night. As luck would have it, the babysitter would be unable to come, so I would have to go with mom to work. It wasn't the first time this had happened, so I wasn't too worried about going with her; I liked it.

After we arrived at mom place of work, she clocked in, then escorted me to the ER secretary. I took a seat next to her as I always did when I went with her. She was a pleasant lady who took great care of me at mom's job. I liked her, she was very sweet, Eventually, she became like my godmother; she was supportive of me and mom outside of work. On this night, however, she noticed the changes in mom's behaviors. Mom was unusually speaking loud, defiant, strange, and her eyes were rolling in the back of her head. The eye rolling was a clear indicator when mom was having a mental breakdown. While it was something I had seen before, and grown quite accustomed to, it was still new to outsiders who didn't understand her condition. I became scared and nervous because, at this point, I had no grandmother to care for me. I felt sick to my stomach, wondering if and how this would end.

Immediately, the ER secretary called the doctor and took me to the staff break area. I didn't know what was happening or what they were doing to my mom. The ER secretary told me to stay put, do not go with anyone or anywhere until she returned back to get me. I obliged her, but my curiosity was getting the best of me. I listened as people tried talking to mom and her attempts to speak back, but nothing made any sense. There was a commotion outside, and my fear grew stronger by the minute. I knew something was off and my gut feeling told me that this would not end well.

Suddenly the noise stopped. I didn't know whether this was good or bad. I couldn't hear my mom voice anymore, and then the ER secretary came back. She saw the fear in my eyes and instantly smiled sweetly at me. She sat across from me, looked me in the eyes and told me that my mom was going to be okay. The doctors would be caring for my mother. An image of mom in the psychiatric hospital in North Carolina came to my mind.

It's crazy how much you remember, even at a young age. I knew that mom was having a mental breakdown again. I began to weep heavily with unending tears. I was alone there with only the secretary. I had no mom, no grandma, and no family to take care of me in that moment. She tried to calm me by holding me in her arms and softly shushing me. I don't remember when I stopped crying, but I vividly remember my mom's boyfriend rushing through the

ER doors. He was the only emergency contact she had listed, so they called him to come pick me up.

On the car ride home, I looked out the window the entire time, sitting in silence as tears rolled down my cheeks. I missed grandma, and I was worried about my mother. The ride felt like it was in slow motion. Suddenly, I was pulled out of my thoughts by my mom's boyfriend touching my shoulder. I jumped and immediately moved closer to the door. I couldn't understand why he was touching me. It was the weekend and images of him beating my mom came into my head, but all he said was, "It's going to be all right, baby. Your mom will be okay, she just needs some rest and for the doctors to take care of her. If you want, we can go to your favorite place to eat, can you guess?"
I watched him, and then reluctantly nodded.

He smiled, "Yes, McDonald's. You want to go?" I nodded and let him take me to McDonald's. It did nothing to make me feel better; but it was my favorite food in an uncomfortable situation.

Once we reached home, I went into my bedroom and immediately began to cry again. Mom's absence was heavy in the apartment. Right then, mom's boyfriend came in again. He said, "You stop that crying, your mom is going to be okay. Now come on, let's get you to bed."

I nodded and wiped my tears. He tucked me in and sat there until I fell asleep. I had never been in this apartment without my mom. It was the coldest eight hours that I had ever had. I didn't even know when I had fallen asleep. I just remember being terrified. All I remember next was that I heard mom's boyfriend calling me and telling me to dress for breakfast. I got out of bed and only then realized it was morning. The apartment smelled of food, and I couldn't help but see what that delicious smell was. I immediately brushed my teeth, washed my face, and went out into the kitchen area. Much to my surprise, I saw that the table was covered with pancakes and omelets. He had cooked up a wonderful breakfast.

Upon finishing our meals, he said to me, "Baby girl, go get your clothes together, okay? We're going to go somewhere." Confusion immediately fell upon my face. He noticed I was hesitant, so he provided further explanation.

"We're going to visit mom, and you're going to stay with your classmate and her family for a little while." The classmate happened to be my new best friend; both of our moms were already great friends.

I went to my room and packed my clothes in my small, pink suitcase. I was scared; I wanted my mom. We left the apartment and went to the hospital to visit mom. We entered the area of the hospital, where I saw her sitting in the corner near a window, rocking herself back and forth, humming. I couldn't help but smile and immediately ran and hugged her. She hugged me back, but she wasn't herself. There was an emptiness in her like she didn't understand where she was at or what was going on. I reassured her that I loved her, but I received no response in return. She looked at me vacantly. It was like the mom that I knew was lost inside of her own mind.

She gazed through me for what seemed like forever. I stared back into her lost eyes, then it was like she just snapped out of it. Maybe it was the familiarity of having her daughter there, or maybe it was a delayed response. All I know is that she began to cry and hugged me again, tighter this time. "I love you too, sweetie," she said between her tears. My voice matched hers, just as small, as I told her I loved her once again.

"You look so much better, mom. Can you come home now?" I said with tears in my eyes. Her boyfriend came and hugged her and kissed her on the forehead. I looked at them as they held hands. Her boyfriend looked like it was a familiar scene to him, seeing mom like this, but he seemed exhausted. I felt a newfound respect for him. Regardless of the fear I had as a child watching mom and him fight, he had grown to become a father figure to me.

After visiting mom, he took me to my friend's house to stay. Her life was so different than mine. While at home, I was used to the whippings and the fights that occurred between mom and her boyfriend. Subconsciously, a part of me thought everything was my fault— the beatings, the mental breakdowns, and the fact that she left me behind in North Carolina. Excitedly at my friend's house there was a sense of calm. Her life was completely opposite than the chaos I'd become accustomed to. It was so surprising to see how she never got beaten for anything, even if she did something wrong.

Her mom and dad were so loving towards me. Whenever I would visit her and spend the night, I would always wonder how rich they were. Unlike us, they lived in a house, together, as a complete family. They were like my second family. They took great care of me, and they made me feel like I was one of their own. They became my saving grace whenever mom became ill.

Eventually, mom and her boyfriend broke up. Though he was great at caring for her even when her mental state wasn't the best, all the drinking and fighting diminished the relationship. As a result, they separated. Still, through all the challenged of being with my mom, he remained a constant in my life. He never had any biological children to my knowledge, he had always and continued he still showed me love and support me as if I was his daughter. He and his new girlfriend would take me to school, shopping, and let me come over and spend time with her children. They became like siblings to me. Although he and my mom's relationship were filled with turmoil, he continued to be respectful and caring toward me long after their relationship was over.

Most people don't understand how difficult it is to have a mentally ill mother. Most of the time, my mother would be ok, but other times, I would have to take up the parenting role. What's worse is the constant paranoia and having to deal with mental anguish and stress. Being too young to truly grasp what it meant, I knew mom was sick, but most of the time, I failed to understand the why of it all.

As I got older, I built resentment toward my mom and her illness. I picked up the tell-tale signs of her not taking her medication and becoming manic, depressed, and stressed. It became easier but not any less stressful. I even became accustomed to being without my grandmother. Of course, it helped when I often called her and my family in the south to update them on everything that was happening. It worried them, but they couldn't do much about it at the time since they didn't live close. But there was a turn of a new leaf when my grandmother, aunt, and one of my favorite cousins relocated to New York for a better life and opportunities. I was relieved that they were coming. I could finally be a child again. It was their turn to deal with her mental health issues.

CHAPTER 3

ALL UNDER ONE ROOF

My grandmother came to live with us, but, by now, her health had deteriorated immensely. She wasn't as lively as she was before and had a difficult time keeping up with everyone. However, she still tried to do the best she could, especially with mom's boyfriend gone. There were now three generations of women in one home. You'd think mom's relationship with her mother would improve. But they had a rough time adjusting, mainly because the roles were reversed. It was mom's job now to take care of her mother while grandma had a habit of bossing us around. Though her health wasn't the best, she still mustered up the strength to do what she could for mom and me.

There was one major plus side to having grandma live with us. Mom's physical abuse became quite less. However, it didn't mean it completely stopped. I recall one time when she told me to take some money to my aunt's house. The total was $100.00 to be exact. I took out $10.00 for snacks at school. Once I reached my aunt's house, I handed her the money, and she counted it. Immediately, she knew about the missing ten dollars. I told her I took it for snacks at school and then walked off. I was ecstatic. It was the best moment of my life because my mom never really gave me snack money. We were not poor, but not rich either; money was tight especially when mom's boyfriend moved out.

I didn't know how bad my day was going to get until my mom called the school. They then called me down to the principal's office and the secretary handed me the phone. I was so scared. I knew what was going to happen to me and what she would do. A part of my childish mind was expecting mom to call the police, but I knew she wouldn't do that. What I feared most was her beatings. When I took the receiver, mom was on the other end, yelling, "You took $10.00 out of your aunt's money?!" Scared, I replied, "No, Mom." My voice was quivering as I whispered into the phone, afraid people would hear me. I spent about two minutes trying to convince her that I must have lost the ten dollars, but she was not going for that lie.

She said, "When you get home, I am going to beat your ass." Then, the line went dead, turning my blood cold. I was terrified as I gave the phone to the school secretary who saw the tears in my eyes. Concerned, she asked me if everything was okay. Fearful, I lied and told her everything was fine. Walking back to my class, I remember thinking that in an instant, the best moment of my life became the worst. I knew it was going to be hell at home, and I wanted to avoid it at any cost.

I came home that day, and grandma wasn't there. Unfortunately, she was in the hospital. As soon as I opened the door, mom was waiting in the living room. She didn't even say hello. All she said was, "Put your stuff in your room, and go get the belt." I was terrified, and I wanted to beg her not to hit me, but I walked to the room while crying hysterically. Mom was walking behind me yelling, "Do not cry now! You were not crying when you stole my money!" I took the belt and handed it to her reluctantly, that's when she began to beat me. It seemed like she beat me for more than thirty minutes or longer while mom was yelling, "Don't cry now, you weren't crying when you stole my money and lied!" I just wanted it to end.

When I look back at it now, I can't help but smirk. It was so silly not to just ask for the money, it definitely could've saved me an unnecessary beating. After she beat the shit out of me, she put the belt away, held me close, and said, *"You know that I love you, tell mom you love her..."* In my mind, I kept repeating how much I hated her but out loud, I had to tell her I loved her. After that, I went to my room and took a nap. I was exhausted and in pain. Just the beating wasn't enough, though. I was also punished for two weeks.

My punishment consisted of going to school, coming home, and going straight to my room. I had to sit in a chair in the corner of my room. I couldn't play with my toys or watch television. I could only read books and write, but nothing else. This would be the pattern for a few years, especially when mom would have a mental breakdown or lose touch with reality. I tried to get used to it, but it wasn't easy. I found tips and tricks, but I harbored a lot of stress and anger within myself. As I grew older, the anger turned into hate.

On one occasion, I remember that it was time to get my report card and my grades weren't all that great. I got scared, but I braced myself for the aftermath. I almost threw it away, but that would make the consequences worse. When I arrived home from school, I gave Mom my report card, and when she opened it, she paused and started yelling, *"You got me paying for this Catholic School, and you're not learning!"*

The same routine was repeated that day, same as always. I got beat, then I went to bed. The only difference this time was that I went to school the next day and I reported it to the school principal. I was not in the mood for two weeks of punishment, sitting in my room by myself and talking to the walls. I told the school, and they called the local Child Protective Services. Once they reached the school, I showed them the swells and red marks from my mom beating me.

It was then I realized that I might be taken away. An immediate fear overcame me as I thought about the repercussions of my words, and I began tearing up. However, when they said that I could not go back home with my mother for a while, I was happy, but the principal, who had become familiar with mom and me, was not happy with the situation at all. She was genuinely concerned about my well-being, and in many ways, she was my angel when I needed one the most. She was a grey-haired, Caucasian lady who wore thin, metal framed glasses and her voice was soft and soothing, offering solace when I had none. Though she didn't know the full ins and outs of our household, she did know how much of a firm parent my mother was. She also knew that mom had mental health issues and how this played a huge part in the way I was being disciplined. Yet and still, I believe that she was getting fed up with the rollercoaster of behaviors.

The child protective worker said that I needed to go with my family members. I cried. I didn't want to go with my aunt. I was secretly still mad at my aunt for saying that I stole the ten dollars, so I told them she was just as abusive as my mother was to me so I wouldn't have to go live with her.

The principal asked if I could go home with her until the child abuse investigation matter was resolved. I stayed with her for two weeks, and I must admit, it was the best two weeks of my young life. During that time, I dealt with no yelling, and I was around someone who was mentally stable. The principal was amazing to me, and a part of me wanted to stay with her indefinitely, but I did miss my mom.

Eventually, when I returned to mom, she was less mean, and seemed a lot calmer. This time, we also moved out of the projects to a bigger apartment. Life seemed to get a little better. However, grandma's health kept getting worse. I remember the horrible day; she had a stroke, and never regained consciousness. I couldn't understand exactly what was happening, but it was very scary and heartbreaking. That day, mom had to make the most hurtful decision in her life. She had to make the decision to remove grandma from life support. I would have never thought that when she went into the hospital, she would never return home.

I have a very vivid memory of that day. All our family gathered at the hospital. I had an empty feeling as I watched my grandma lying lifeless on the bed. She was my protector, my guardian angel, and now she was gone. After grandma passed, my mom had a mental breakdown. Without her mother, this was the first time she understood how much her mom meant to her, regardless of how much they didn't get along.

When we settled back into our new normal, a new apartment, and no grandmother, mom and I began to get along. This time, she had a new boyfriend. He was a gentle guy. He and mom never fought, and he was genuinely nice. Because of her condition, mom would get verbally abusive, but he hung in there with her. By now, mom had a mental health caseworker, a therapist, and others who checked in throughout the month to ensure that she was mentally stable. Through all of this, she was finally getting better, and things were looking optimistic.

CHAPTER 4

CHAOS BRINGS CHANGE

Things were too good to be true because it wasn't long after that everything began to change again. It was during summer, and I was going to camp. That evening, I didn't come home on time. To this day, I can't understand why I did some things knowing my mom had zero tolerance for nonsense. I guess all the years of dealing with mom's mental illness and the harsh discipline brought my rebellious streak to the forefront. I began to act out.

I came in, and mom had been drinking. She was not a drinker, but when she did, she would yell at me. This time, it was about not cleaning my closet. Very rudely, I told her that it was, in fact, clean. I called her out that day, asking her why she always yelled and complained. My tolerance of coping with my mother's mental illness had taken a toll this day. In hindsight, I don't know what possessed me to do that, but all hell broke loose.

Suddenly, I saw her flying out of the chair and grabbing her belt. She whooped me so much that I ran into the pantry, trying to get away from her. As she continued to beat me, I was trying to climb under a ladder, and she struck my hand. I immediately moved my hand away, and I hit my finger so hard on the pantry shelf that I sprained it. Mom didn't stop though, she kept swinging until she got tired. Once it was over, I repeated the normal routine and took a nap. After the beatings, I would never want to eat anything, I just wanted to sleep.

The next day my finger was swollen as I made my way to summer camp. I tried to hide it, but my camp counselor saw how I was moving my hand and asked what happened. I didn't refrain this time, I told her that my mom had beaten me. I instantly regretted it, remembering what had happened the last time but the deed was already done. She reported it to her supervisor, and again, Child Protective Services was called.

This time was different because the Child Protective Services was familiar with my mom. They told me again that I had to live with someone else. I was over the dynamics of my childhood. I refused to live with family or friends. So, I was put in an emergency shelter, and from there, we would go back and forth to family court. When I was at the shelter, I found out that mom had a mental breakdown. I felt terrible because I'm sure this one was because of the trauma of losing me, along with not having her mother with her. I won't say it was easy for me either, I missed my grandmother, and my mom terribly, regardless of how much she beat me.

The next ninety days seemed quite long, filled with anguish and uncertainty. I didn't know what was waiting for me. I loved my mother. When I thought about it, it didn't matter how much she beat me. I was her only child and the love of her life, as she was for me. I began to feel sorry for everything that I did. I began to think that I should have lied. I shouldn't have told them about my mom and her beatings. However, the anger had gotten the best of me, and the stress was making it so much worse to be at home.

After months of evaluating our case, we finally went to court— one of many times. This time, however, it was different. I was brought in by the shelter staff, and that's where I saw mom. I was beyond happy. I ran to her and gave her the biggest hug. I noticed how different she looked; how much sadness was in her eyes. I felt heartbroken and guilty. In this moment that's when I realized that I should've stayed quiet. Maybe, just maybe, I could've been at home with mom if I had.

The court room was intimate, composed of a sitting area with two tables—one for the Department of Children and Family Services representative and one for the child and their representative. The walls were off-white and like most courtrooms, there was rich-colored, mahogany furniture. The judge who was an older, chunky Caucasian man with gray hair, sat up high in his seat with the stenographer near him—the bailiff was nearby as well. I looked around the room at every person who could affect the outcome of my destiny. The minutes of waiting seemed like forever. Finally, the judge finished studying the documents before him, then removed his glasses and spoke.

"Natasha, we spoke to your mom."

As soon as my mom heard that, she began to cry. I could sense the sadness and stress in her, though I couldn't understand what was happening. I too began to cry out of confusion and fear. The judge continued, despite our cries of desperation.

"We've given your mom the option to agree that you will go into foster care, or I have instructed her I would terminate her rights. She has agreed and signed the paperwork for you to go into foster care indefinitely."

I couldn't believe it. My world was torn apart. I would no longer have the daily bond I shared with my mom. I was all alone, all because I went to the Child Protective Service. I lost my mom that day. I knew nothing would ever be the same again.

CHAPTER 5

A WARD OF THE COURT: PART 1

Though I never really pictured my life without them, I did often wonder what it would be like without my mom, grandma, or family. My thoughts became reality only after I got tired of my mom beating me. I can't act like it was all bad though. It's not that I didn't love my mom—there's never been a moment in time that I didn't. I know she loved me too, which made me reflect on the good things in my life. We had a nice apartment and food to eat every day. Though my clothes were not designer, they were new and clean. But even with all these blessings, my mother's mental breakdowns took a toll on her, and in a way, it broke me down as well.

I used to wonder what it would be like without the constant screams, the beatings, and frequent worries about her health. At one point, I thought leaving mom would be a good decision. It would give me a decent life away from the abuse. What did I know back then? I was just a kid. I stood in a courtroom with my world being torn apart. I was forced to deal with the consequences of my actions.

My mind wasn't ready to accept my new reality without mom; I was just too numb. I don't particularly remember all of what happened in the courtroom that day, but I do remember the chaos, and mostly, the distress on my mother's face that day. It was difficult to see her eyes welled with tears, crying uncontrollably. I couldn't understand it, our special bond was broken. I wanted to hold her and go home with her, but I couldn't.

Someone had taken me out of the courtroom. I didn't know who it was, but all I knew was that the glimpse of my mom was drifting away from me. I wanted to scream and cry, but my body refused to react. I was standing amongst so many people, all of them well dressed and all of them with somber looks on their faces. I couldn't even run away.

Even though the door was right there, it was locked from the inside. However, just as the idea came into my head, a woman walked up to me and smiled the sweetest smile imaginable. Yet, all I wanted to do was run. She kneeled in front of me and told me I was being given a few minutes to say goodbye to my mom. I never voiced it but all I could think was, *how do you say goodbye to your own mother?*

I felt my mother's presence behind me, and I turned to see her. I saw my aunt hug her as she wept, and her heartbreak was evident from her eyes. It was never my intention to hurt my mom, I loved her unconditionally. All I wanted was for her to stop beating me. Yet, in that instant, I would gladly have given her the right to hit me if it meant going home with her again. I couldn't stop the tears, and neither could she.

I remember it vividly. She took me and hugged me tightly. I felt her arms around me, and I took a mental note to remember what it felt like. I remember her head resting on mine as she held me close to her. I saw my aunt's hands were resting on both of my mom's shoulders, gripping them to hold her back. She held me so tight that I could feel my mom's heart pounding.

Quietly, she whispered in my ear, "Why, baby? I love you in the name of Jesus!" She whispered it at least three times, like a recording set on play. All I could say to her was, "I love you, Mom."

Just as I did, the bubble of guilt and pain burst, and we both erupted into fresh tears again. I had really screwed up, and there was no turning back this time. I could've stayed in that position forever, but then a hand touched my shoulders and gently pull me back. My mom gripped me tighter, and I held her. But it was no use, and before I knew it, I was being dragged away.

I remember looking at my mom as my eyes filled with sadness. Her image blurred with my tears as the distance grew between us. Her sobs died down behind me as I was taken away. I distinctly remember watching her leave the court with my aunt. I was alone now. As I looked down the long corridor, I noticed that the people had dispersed, and the court was almost empty. My footsteps echoed in the hallway, as the lady led me to a cold metal bench. She told me to sit down, and I did. I was scared, my body felt like jelly. I was completely numb.

I sat there on the bench for what felt like hours. I was entirely alone with my thoughts. I could not believe the mess I had created. There was no turning back. A part of me wished my mom would come out and say it was all a joke, but another part of me knew that was not happening. I had so many thoughts racing through my mind. I was calling myself names, such as stupid and crazy, sitting there dumbfounded and alone. I controlled the urge not to take my hand and bang it on my head. My whole life had changed just because I was mad at my mom.

After thirty minutes or so, I heard the door opening and the click of heels on the ground. I looked up to see two ladies walk out of what I assumed was their office, but I wasn't sure. One of the ladies had unbelievably soft features. Her hair was black and pulled up in a bun. She looked important.

I remember being so scared. I didn't know where I would be going or what would happen. She came closer to me. When we were face-to-face, she bent down to speak to me at eye level.

"Natasha, you are going with Ms. Yvonne. She will take you to another local shelter for girls. There you will stay for approximately 30 days for evaluations until your placement into a permanent foster home."

I did not understand anything, but I heard the word 'foster home' and began crying all over again with snot running down my nose. I didn't bother looking up at the other woman, but I softly replied with all the energy I could muster up, *"Ye..ye..yes, ma'am."*

Ms. Yvonne came and grabbed my hand. Together, we walked down the hall that led to the back of the building. My chest tightened. Mom always told me not to trust strangers, but here was a stranger leading me to a big white van. I heard horror stories, about kid shelters and foster homes... I was terrified. I would hear unimaginable things like foster parents starving children, locking them in rooms, and shelters where the kids were bullied, and the staff were mean. Though all these thoughts swarmed my head, there was nowhere to run to. Ms. Yvonne opened the door, and I had no choice but to get in.

Upon entering the van, I heard talking and moving. I saw three girls and two boys... all of them seemed to be terrified. This made me even more scared and nervous. I could not get my mother out of my mind. I needed her so bad that I wanted to jump out of the van. My mind was on a constant repeat. I couldn't help but to continuously think, *how the hell could I do this to my mother?!*

In my heart of hearts, I knew mom loved me. Even though she would often beat me, I never wanted to be taken away; I just wanted my mother to stop. Soon, Ms. Yvonne closed the door, and another lady said hello to everyone in the van. It was all a blur to me, like a bad dream.

"Hello, I am Mrs. Tina, and I will be one of your counselors at the shelter where you will live for a few weeks." She sounded strict, like an angry principal. Much like Ms. Yvonne, she was very professional. I could tell they took their jobs seriously.

Ms. Yvonne told everyone to put on their seat belts, not to get up, and not to ask any questions while she was driving. I couldn't help but remember how I would mouth off when my mother gave those same instructions. But Ms. Yvonne was not my mother, and I didn't want her to speak to me at all. However, I held my tongue because I didn't know those people or what they would do to me if I were to get smart. I felt caged and afraid; there was no way out. I sat in my seat almost frozen, not being able to move anywhere.

As I looked out the window, wondering where my next destination would be, I realized that my mom and I had traveled these streets. But somehow, they seemed unfamiliar to me. They had a sinister, unrecognizable aspect to them which made me feel like I did not belong. It was suffocating, but I tried to stay calm.

Suddenly, we pulled into a short winding driveway and then came to a complete stop. My heart was pounding so fast in my chest that I felt I could not breathe. It seemed like someone was sucking the air out of my lungs. It felt like I was having an asthma attack and needed my inhaler. I remembered packing it, but I could not find it after frantically searching my backpack. I took a deep breath, then realized the asthma pump was in my pocket. I pulled it out and took three quick puffs. I looked out the window and presumed we'd arrived at our destination. When I stood up to get a better look, I heard Ms. Tina's voice booming, "Sit down, young lady."

Her voice sent shivers down my spine; I sat down immediately upon her request. The door opened, and the young boys were told to get off the bus. I was confused. Why was it just the boys? Why weren't we getting off? Ms. Tina closed the door, and we began driving again. In my mind, I kept wondering why we were not getting off. I became frightened. The other girls and I were looking at each other with a questioning stare. None of us had the guts to open our mouths, but you could tell we all were thinking the same thing.

As the door closed, Ms. Yvonne spoke again. "Okay, ladies, time to get you home. Make sure you keep your seat belt on."

Nothing made sense then, but later, I found out that we dropped the boys to the male shelter. As we rode off, I felt overwhelmed, scared, and guilty, as any child would in my situation. The nervous energy was strong in that van, it was filled with fear and pain. As a child, I felt insecure, even though my mom dealt with mental illness. Her parenting may have been strict, but she was still my security blanket.

As a kid, you really don't understand what being a parent involves. All you know is that someone older than you is telling you what to do every day. Just like most children, I didn't understand the complexities of adulthood. I thought being older just equated to more experiences and knowledge, and the power to make decisions for kids like me.

After dropping the boys off at the shelter, we drove into a great neighborhood in a small-town. As I looked out the window, I saw a big white house, and we pulled into its driveway. My fear somehow dissipated and I felt a little more at ease. I was in awe by the view of the house; coming from a low-income housing and urban America, it was a major change for me.

The house had a beautiful large landscape outside with lush green lawns and patches of various flowers. The house was completely white, almost gleaming in the sunlight. It looked like pure perfection, and my eyes widened at the sight before me. I kept looking out, thinking this was too good to be true. There were so many horror stories out there about shelters. I heard Ms. Yvonne's voice as she told us all to take off the seat belt and carefully get out of the van.

As the door opened, one by one, every one of us got out and waited for Ms. Tina or Ms. Yvonne to lead us into the "White House." I felt a little calm then, especially as we walked towards the house in a line. Up close, I noticed that the house really wasn't all that flawless – the door was big but old with several cracks in it, and the paint was chipping off in some places. The door squeaked a little when it opened and had to be pushed for it to open completely.

Everyone else went ahead of me, but I stood outside, looking up at the big house. This house almost seemed like a dream, but it was a nightmare. As soon as I walked in the door, my anxiety began again. I could feel my heart racing and beads of sweat began forming on my forehead. As soon as I stepped inside, Ms. Tina reached over to me to close the door. I looked around the house and it was very nice inside, but it still looked old. We all stood in a line and looked in front of us at a lady wearing a green dress.

"Hello, ladies. Welcome! I am Mrs. Jackson. Put your stuff down and relax. I am sure you have had a long day, and you're nervous,..." She looked at each of us with a smile on her face and continued, "...but it's okay. Everything will be all right. Now put your things down so that you can have some lunch."

Mrs. Jackson was sweet. She looked and reminded me of grandma. It was perhaps because she was older, and her voice was raspy, but it put your mind at ease. In my childhood days, I'd watched the Jeffersons and the Archie Bunker show faithfully, and

Mrs. Jackson's voice reminded me of Louise Jefferson. She was always giving out lessons. She spoke from a caring place, but she did not hold anything back. To her the truth was the truth. While she had a calm demeanor, she spoke with a firm tone.

We were led to what I thought was the dining room and we were seated at the long, wooden table. I looked around and saw the sunlight streaming in through the windows, overlooking the scenery outside. Smells of delicious food entered the room, and I looked back to see the table being set. We all sat down and enjoyed a late lunch which, I must say, was very tasty.

After lunch, we were taken to a steep, narrow, stairway. Scared, I gripped the railing tightly. Even though the food had made me sluggish, I pushed myself to walk carefully up the stairs, following Ms. Tina's lead. All I could think about was my mother and what she was doing at that moment. I thought about our routine and how much I missed her. I fought the sob rising in my throat and moved forward.

We reached the top of the stairs towards the short hallway. Ms. Tina stayed in front of us, guiding us to our rooms. I was nervous. I didn't know what to expect, but I certainly couldn't expect my own room like back home. Ms. Tina opened a door and led me inside. I looked around. The room was nicer than expected. It had two beds and seemed cozy. There was a small window between the beds to allow the sunlight in, and the walls were painted light pink.

Ms. Tina assigned another young girl and I to the room. My first thought was about how I went from having my own room to having a roommate. Once again, the guilt of my actions sunk in, as the familiar lump rose in my throat. Ms. Tina and Ms. Yvonne came to each room to inventory the little number of items we had. They told us that our family would be able to drop off clothing and personal items in a few days. My heart skipped at the thought of seeing mom again, but I tried to be as calm as possible.

Once the items were inventoried completely, we went back downstairs and lingered around trying to familiarize ourselves with the house. Everything felt so new; it was difficult getting used to it. All we could do was wait for instructions. The day was passing by, and the strangeness of the new place was only growing.

Eventually, Ms. Jackson asked us all to sit at the dining table, as we took a seat, she began to go over the rules. I couldn't concentrate on her words. My mind wandered off towards a broken part inside of me. I was thinking about my mom, how she must be crying, and it broke my heart. I knew that wherever she was, she was still crying. A part of me also knew that she wouldn't be able to take the strain. This would be enough to cause a mental breakdown. I just didn't know when it would happen, but I was certain that a mental breakdown was underway. Every now and then, Ms. Jackson's voice traveled through the cracks of my thoughts, and I vaguely heard her assign us chores, scheduled bedtimes, times when we could call our families, and daily house meeting after dinner clean-up.

Once Ms. Jackson told us everything that we needed to know, she led us towards the living room. Some of us watched TV while others took brief naps. Silence and numbness filled the air; the day was sad and surreal for most of us. I looked around at the other girls and noticed how none of us were old enough to properly deal with this situation. We were entering a stage in our life where complete strangers would start making decisions for us and telling us what to do. It was a dark thought.

I watched television, but my mind was lost, I didn't know what was happening. The room felt cold, sterile, and incomplete, with no family or familiar items. All we had was a lot of uncertainty. As the TV played, the actors' words would catch our attention from time to time, and we would laugh, more like chuckle slightly. None of us really had it in us to laugh, or even smile. It was quiet in the room, almost calming. However, that calmness was suddenly disturbed when outside we began to hear quick movements and commotion. We all looked at each other, confused, and mouthed, *"What's going on?"*

The confused shrugs prevented any answer.

Suddenly, the door opened, and Mrs. Jackson appeared along with two ladies who she introduced as Ms. Grace and Ms. Diana. We were told that they were the evening staff responsible for our care. I watched the women intently, never once feeling safe or comfortable. The only time I felt comfortable was if my mother decided to visit, but I never knew ahead of time when that would happen.

The women all spoke back and forth, but I didn't catch their conversations. I only heard Ms. Diana call my name and I turned and looked. Eventually, all I could muster out was a 'yes' to everything she was saying. In hindsight, I could have answered her more quickly; but honestly, I was all out of niceness. It had been a long day for me already. Ms. Diana asked if I would like to help prepare dinner. I looked at her, fighting the urge to say no, and responded with a 'yes.' What else would I say anyway? I already knew what would happen if I ever said no to my mother, and I was in no mood to find out what would happen if I said it to Ms. Diana.

As soon as I said it, Ms. Diana, another girl, and I proceeded to the kitchen. We watched Ms. Diana and followed her every move, trying to prepare the food accordingly. Throughout the entire time, she also lectured us about how she didn't want us to be the type of kids who stayed in trouble for the rest of our lives. It was evident that she had given this speech more than once. Ms. Diana assured us that we would be okay. She said to follow the rules, listen to the adults, and stay out of trouble.

After a while, dinner was ready. Successfully, the three of us had prepared spaghetti, and everyone enjoyed the meal. I must admit, dinner was good, and spaghetti is still my favorite today. We cleaned up after dinner and sat for our required house meeting. It was the first house meeting I had ever had.

In an African American household, we never had family or house meetings. Our elders "said what they meant and meant what they said" and you listened and followed instructions. No one cared about a child's feelings. This is what set the tone for how my mother disciplined me. It was all she knew. During our meeting, we were asked questions about how we felt about being in a shelter. They asked us about our feelings towards house rules, and what we expected from this experience. I gladly answered all those questions with the response of 'I hate it, even though it's nice,' and, 'I miss my mother.'

I didn't really care about the rules because the chores and cleaning were my mother's obsession anyway. As the meeting ended, we were given toiletries, some clothing for those of us who didn't have certain items, and we were allowed to go shower and relax. I could tell by the exhaustion on everyone's faces that all the girls desperately needed a shower. It wasn't because we were physically tired, but the mental stress of this whole ordeal was overwhelming.

By 8:30 PM, we were all in bed and relaxing. According to the rules, our bedtime was at 9:30 PM, and the lights were out at 10:30 PM. I don't think any of us cared if they turned the lights off at 8:30 PM that night. That's how drained a bunch of pre-teens were. We were all still in shock that we were in a place with complete strangers on unfamiliar territory.

That night, as I laid in my bed, I stared at the walls, the ceiling, and anywhere my eyes landed. It was cold and warm at the same time if that's possible. I felt hot, but my heart was frozen with fear. Being in a completely new place around completely new people without my mom was a fear I couldn't describe. More than the rest, I was more stressed in the dark.

I don't remember when, but I must have fallen asleep some time while staring at the ceiling. All I remember next is seeing the hint of sunlight streaming in from the window. That was the only indication I had of sleep and what I thought was going to be a long night seemed short. I must have slept well because I don't recall falling asleep or waking up throughout the night.

As I lie in bed, my eyes not ready to open for the new day, I heard a voice. It definitely wasn't one of the girls, but it was a lady telling us to wake up. I heard the light steps approaching and then the squeak of the opening door. She saw me already sitting up in my bed and greeted me with a smile.

"Good morning, I am Ms. Ruby, the overnight staff," she said gently.

I greeted her back but said nothing else. I was in no mood to make morning introductions. As if she were there, I heard my mom's voice in my head telling me as she always did, "Brush your teeth before you talk to people early in the morning."

Keeping that in mind, I got out of bed and proceeded out of the room towards the bathroom. Something so simple became a surreal experience, but the staff was caring and pleasant. I honestly didn't expect it, then again, I had just gotten here. All the shelter horror stories I heard kept echoing in my head. I tried my best to not focus on it. I completed my morning hygiene routine up; went down to eat breakfast. As we ate our food a familiar voice came through the door.

We all greeted Ms. Jackson together. As soon as she walked in, we felt safe. I really didn't know why, we met her less than twenty-four hours ago. I suppose it was the friendly grandmother vibes she gave off which made us feel at ease. However, under no circumstances did she make me feel as safe as my grandmother did. It's true what they say, the love of your family is unmatched. It was for me because my grandmother was instrumental in raising me. Regardless of the situation, she knew exactly how to make me feel better.

Ms. Jackson informed us that we would be going to school at the boy's shelter. It was regulated by law for children to gain an education, whether in a shelter or foster care. As Ms. Jackson finished talking, Ms. Yvonne and Ms. Tina walked in, and we all politely greeted them. Ms. Yvonne told us to go to the van so we could leave for school, which was about forty minutes away. None of the girls interacted with each other and we all quietly loaded in the van. The door closed and it began to move. I stared out the window as the radio played. I had no direct thoughts, but I was mentally somewhere far away. I think, subconsciously, I was trying to cope and process my emotions.

I looked out as the sun kissed my face, the blur of the buildings disappearing from my sight. I was lost in my thoughts when we arrived at the boy's shelter and only realized it when the van stopped. Ms. Tina stepped off, and we all got out of the van. We followed Ms. Tina into the home. It was a big house – it seemed at least three times bigger than the girl's shelter. Later I learned that the house was the headquarters for the administrators, case managers, and other personnel, which explained it's size. As soon as we entered, it was as if all of us stopped at once and lightly bumped into each other.

Slowly, smiles spread on each of our faces as we looked at the boys sitting in the area. Though some boys paid no attention, most of them stared and smirked at us. A lady and a gentleman came out of the front doors of the home. They both dressed sensibly and walked with a purpose. They stood in front of us and introduced themselves as Mr. Daryl and Ms. Linda.

Mr. Daryl was tall with a deep voice. He scanned the area and addressed each of us with his eyes before speaking. "I need you all to listen up. We are going to class, and I don't want any problems from anyone today."

Following his lead, Ms. Tina chimed in and told everyone to follow her. As she walked, her heels clicked, and we all proceeded down the hall into the back of the building until we reached a small area. I would not say it was a traditional classroom, but it provided an environment to learn. There were proper tables and chairs, and a chalkboard in front of the room.

The first day was eventful and quite different from regular school. As it ended, we gathered all our items, put them away and went back to the shelter. I was tired because I hadn't been to school for a few weeks. I had been in an emergency shelter which wasn't near my home school district.

I was also placed under strict court supervision. This included counseling sessions, as well as visiting medical and psychological professionals. The psychological visits were court ordered due to the attempted suicide when I was a child. Yes, you heard me right. I tried to take my life which required me to be hospitalized. I was tired of mom beating me. It was unbearable at times, and I thought the only chance I would be free of the physical abuse; if I were dead.

The routine mom and I had was normal to me, whether good or bad. This made it extremely difficult to adjust to my 'new normal.' As the days went by, I became homesick and depressed, but overtime, I began to get used to it. I even liked spending my time there. I was supposed to be at the shelter for only 30 days. However, my time was extended to 60 days. Honestly, I didn't really mind it. Though I missed mom, my family, and friends, I didn't miss getting beaten. I got to know the other girls and eventually befriended them too. I found out that they had far more tragic events in life compared to mine.

My roommate's mom was a drug addict. She was also sexually assaulted by a family member. Hearing their stories and then thinking of mine, I would cry at night. I often wondered how mothers could allow this to happen to their children. My mom had a mental illness, but what I could say with certainty was that she would never knowingly let anyone harm me. I was her prized possession. Even though she had questionable disciplining skills, she would still never let anyone deliberately hurt me.

It was court time again, the judge always wanted updates on the kids every 30 days. He also wanted to see and speak with us. I had already been to court for an update hearing before. I knew the court routine, so I thought today was no different than any other court visit. The usual people were there. I was still nervous, but not as nervous as the first time. This time, I knew the routine and was prepared for it. The judge asked me how I was doing and asked whether I wanted to tell him anything. I politely said, "No, judge." At that time, I didn't know anything about how to address the judge. The only thing I knew was that he was important and made all the decisions.

After speaking to me, the judge asked the other people questions as well. Due to this being the standard routine, I didn't pay much attention to anyone—I was use to my court appointments going this way. However, one woman stood up that I had never seen before. She immediately diverted my attention, and I started to listen.

"Your Honor, I am from the foster care agency. We have agreed to accept the ward into our care."

I didn't really know much about how the courts worked, but I knew that once a child entered the court system, they became a "Ward of the Court," which meant that the court was responsible for minors, and the judge made the final decision on all aspects of a minor's life. The moment I heard about foster care; I went numb all over again from the shock. I can't describe the feeling. It was as if I were losing something all over again. Even though I knew the shelter was temporary. In some strange way, it had become a safe place to live. The staff was great, the other girls were not bad at all, and hell, I hadn't even gotten beaten in months! Finally, I feel like I was in an okay place my life.

A WARD OF THE COURT: PART 2

This was going to be another change. I hoped it was going to be for the best and I knew the shelter wouldn't be my final abode. However, I wasn't prepared to go through the change again. Any kind of move is traumatic for a child, especially when they are not prepared. I returned to the shelter that day, but this time, I was heading there with a new feeling. I returned nervously for the next phase of this process. I remained there another few days while the foster care agency finalized my placement arrangements.

I would have moments where I wished I could stay in the shelter forever. It had become my new home. I had come to trust the staff, and befriend the girls there, and best of all, the neighborhood was safe. Weeks went by and every day became just as heartbreaking as when I first came here. After weeks, it was finally time to leave the shelter. I woke up that morning and went about my routine. While nothing was wrong, I still felt somber. I sat down to eat, saw Mrs. Jackson and all my pent-up energy was released. I began to cry hysterically. Ms. Jackson came over and asked me what was wrong.

I looked at her and saw the face that had comforted me the first day I arrived. With tears running down my cheeks, I told her, "I don't want to leave here; nor do I want to go to a foster home. I want to stay here with you, your staff, and the girls."

I hiccupped and sobbed. People kept getting ripped from my life and I couldn't stand the thought of losing more people. Ms. Jackson chuckled and said with a smile, "Baby, we don't want you to go either, but our job here is done. You must go to a more suitable family environment. The shelter is not meant for kids to live in forever."

She suddenly became somber as well and, with a sad smile, said, "We aren't kicking you out, honey. You're not one of the ones we kicked out." I held every word she said close to my heart. I never knew that Ms. Jackson would become the most important person to me at the shelter. She was the supervisor; and eventually, she became my go-to person whenever I had a problem.

I recall my mom's first visit to the to the shelter and the role Ms. Jackson played in it. As much as I missed mom, I couldn't help but lash out at her. I remember saying, "Mom, you need to get me back home." I desperately wanted my old life back and needed the familiarity.

Mom didn't understand my frustration. She answered, "I didn't put you in here. You got the white man in our family business, so you sit here until the judge lets you out."

I got angry, I knew she could not hit me, so I began yelling at her, "It's all your fault. You should have stopped beating me and having mental breakdowns. Then I wouldn't even have left."

Mrs. Jackson hit the corner of the dining room wall and immediately said, "If you disrespect your mother again, you will lose all your special privileges as long as you're in here." I stopped instantly and walked away from my mom. I went to my room and didn't come back out until she was gone. From Mrs. Jackson's tone, I questioned whether she kicked kids out for being disrespectful. It created an uneasy feeling in the pit of my stomach.

I was still crying. Ms. Jackson came close to me and put a hand on my shoulder, saying, "Baby, you go to your new home. You behave, be nice and polite to your foster family, and always be loving and respectful to your mother when she visits, or I will come to your foster home."

A new day rolled in, and we had just completed our hygiene and breakfast routine. Soon after, I heard a knock on the door, and I knew that whoever it was, they had come to take me away. Just then, Ms. Yvonne open the door and greet the woman while another voice greeted her back. I didn't want to move. My body went cold, knowing that it was time.

As the lady entered, Ms. Yvonne called my name and Ms. Jackson was there the whole time, holding my hand. Ms. Yvonne introduced the woman and told me that her name was Ms. Mary Alice and that she was taking me to my new home. I eyed her up and down, and my first thought was how she had nerdy hippie qualities. She was not dressed like all the other social workers or court professionals. She had a long flowing shirt and skirt. Her hair was curly, and she had round bi-focal glasses.

I could hear the clock ticking in my head, and soon, I was told to say goodbye to everyone. I didn't want to, but I had to. I gave everyone hugs and said my goodbyes; I cried the most when I hugged Ms. Jackson. However, the strangest thing happened when I was leaving. When I hugged Ms. Yvonne; my eyes grew watery again. She was the type of woman I thought I would harbor feelings of resentment toward. Throughout my stay at the shelter, Ms. Yvonne was the one you didn't play with. She was what I imagined a father figure would be like.

Ms. Yvonne was firm but fair. I had never seen her emotional, but I was when she said to me, "You be good and do remarkable things with yourself." Her words triggered emotions of sadness and anxiety in me. I wanted to hug her and never let her go. Nevertheless, I waved goodbye and proceeded to get into Ms. Mary Alice's car. I looked back and kept watching the people I had come to love so much in just over two months.

As Ms. Mary Alice began to drive, I kept my eyes fixed on the people I got to know so well. Now here I was riding off again with another stranger, leaving the nice, landscaped building that had been my home over the last few months. Everything and everyone began to disappear as the distance grew. I fought the urge to cry again as my eyes took in the last bit of the place I was leaving behind. There were so many times when I wondered what would have happened if I had not gone through this process, and never went through the court system.

Who else would I have had other than Aunt Jodye? As far as I saw, no family member's, other than one aunt, ever came to any of my court dates. Even though my mom lost custody, she still attended my court meetings, parenting classes, and all other requirements. My aunt had taken care of me; along with my grandmother when we lived in North Carolina. Since the passing of my grandmother, my aunt became the matriarch of our family. Though she was stern, she grew to become my favorite aunt.

The reason I couldn't stay with my aunt was that, while my aunt did not have mental illness, she still had the same disciplinary tactics as my mother; I was very vocal to the judge about not wanting to live with her. To be honest, I think the judge and my aunt would have had a verbal altercation if I lived with her. She said exactly what she wanted, to who she wanted, and when she wanted.

She was the strongest, most hard-working Black woman that I knew. I have a lot of her leadership qualities in me and her ability to deal with all the obstacles that life threw at her. It's my belief that the judge set the stage for me to be the strong independent woman that I am. Shelter life is not something any child should have to endure. Even though my experience was not the worst, it was still a lonely, heart-wrenching moment. Every time I think about it now, I know that it truly does, "take a village to raise a child." In my case, so many unrelated individuals had a hand in who I have become.

However, in my biological family village, no one stepped up to ensure that my relationship with my mom remained happy and safe. To this day, I don't resent any of my family. I love them all the same. I wish that funding, support, and services were readily accessible to families in need. This would provide children with stability and natural support from within their own family village. In return, this could prevent families from being torn apart.

CHAPTER 6

HOME SWEET FOSTER HOME

When it came time for me to leave the shelter, I felt nothing except sadness and loneliness. I also harbored a lot of resentment for everyone. I was age twelve by the time I reached foster care and I had gone through a lot already. I'd simply had enough of everyone at such an early age, and I didn't want any more of the decisions to be made by the court. I went into survival mode.

Throughout the car ride to the foster home, all I could think about was going through all the hurdles thrown at my little life. I fantasized about adulthood… a time when I would be able to take control over my own life and make my own decisions. As a child, you think being an adult is easy, but once you become an adult, things are even harder, and more responsibilities follow.

When we arrived at my new foster home, I didn't expect the surprise that awaited me. My mom's home was just around the corner. At that moment, I put my hand on the door handle, thought about jumping out of the car, and running as fast as I could to my mom's house, but I didn't. Instead, I looked out at the pink-reddish house that stood in between a great landscape and the number "241" written on the home.

That house would become one of the most significant places in my life. It would be the blueprint of who I am today. It offered both good and bad experiences, and that is something I can never let go of. Although, back then, I hated it. I absolutely appreciated living at "241." When our car stopped in front of the house, I was in awe. I moved closer to the window and looked at the magnificence in front of us. Ms. Mary Alice quickly came around, opened the door, and we got my things out of the car.

Together, we walked up to the front porch and knocked. I didn't know what awaited me on the other side of the door, and I was a little nervous. Once the door opened and we stepped onto the front porch, a voice greeted us. A short, stout 60-year-old lady with grey hair stood in front of us. She spoke well and had the prettiest smile. My first impression of her was that she was a kind-hearted woman, but I couldn't be too sure.

Ms. Mary Alice had filled me in about her during our drive, and she mentioned how my foster mother's family had a tragic accident in the 70's. It required her to take custody of five children, who were her relatives. She did it without any hesitation. This would be the first step in Aunt Jodye becoming a foster parent.

"Hello ladies, come on in!" Aunt Jodye said happily upon us entering the house.

As we followed her into the home, nervousness set in. I missed the people who had become my second family, and I was a little scared of my future there as well. I didn't even notice how beautiful the house was.

"I am Aunt Jodye, and you are, young lady?" she asked as she walked ahead. She occasionally turned back to smile at me.

"Natasha," I said in a faint voice, adopting a careless demeanor. I couldn't help but treat this as just another temporary stay. I was not in the mood for a new aunt. Hell, I only had one biological aunt that took an interest in mom and me. I was not at all interested in any conversation that was going on, nor was I being respectful and polite to "Aunt Jodye."

As my nervousness settled, my mind was simply occupied with how beautiful the foster home was. It looked like something right out of a magazine. I looked around, impressed by the chandeliers, velvet carpet, and the dinner table set with formal dinnerware. It was so much better than the shelter, but I still had no intentions of being nice to Aunt Jodye. All I thought was, *"Hell! She's not my mom!"*

Aunt Jodye had us sit down at the dining table. I sat in a chair while Ms. Mary Alice and Aunt Jodye tried to engage me in a conversation that revolved around me. After about an hour of conversing, it was time for Ms. Mary Alice to leave. I remember how I did not even say goodbye to her. I know that as a 12-year-old I was being very rude. I was honestly tired of people coming and going in my life. I had given Ms. Mary Alice and my other caseworker, Ms. Olivia, a tough time.

I could not see that their intention was to help me. I guess the separation from my mother had created insecurity in me, along with trust and abandonment issues, some of which I still have today. As soon as Ms. Mary Alice left, another lady walked in and greeted us. She was the lady who showed me to my room. I would later see how much we wouldn't get along. Initially, I thought she was Aunt Jodye's daughter, but it turned out that she was someone Aunt Jodye had taken in. I was quite impressed when I learned how Aunt Jodye had taken in and helped a lot of people like ex-cons, drug addicts, women in abusive relationships, and anyone who asked for assistance.

When we reached my room, I looked around and then put my stuff on the floor. I felt indignant and I didn't refrain from showing it. After putting my things in the room, I sat in a chair by Aunt Jodye's bedroom. I didn't want to interact with anyone, neither did I want to stay there. I was sitting minding my business when the lady who showed me to my room started to head out. She asked if I wanted to go with her. I said no, and that was when Aunt Jodye interjected and said, "Honey, stop looking so mean, this is your new home and family. You should go outside, you been in a shelter for weeks, get some fresh air." She seemed genuinely nice, and there was nothing much to do inside anyways, so I did as she suggested.

We were out for a few hours, and I admit, it felt good. I didn't know I needed the fresh air as much as I did. When we returned to Aunt Jodye's home, I walked in, and she asked if I was okay. I simply said yes and sat down. As we spoke, a girl came into the living room. I met her when I lived with my mom. Her name was Kema. As soon as she saw me, she shouted, "I know her, Aunt Jodye! That's my friend. We rode the bus together and attended the same camp!" I was excited as well. Seeing a familiar face comforted me, and I finally felt like I was somewhere safe. Immediately, we hugged and started talking.

Eventually we went in the room and unpacked my stuff. Aunt Jodye came into my room, looked at the few clothes I had, and said, "Baby, you don't have any clothes." She seemed so concerned. All I could do was nod. I didn't know what the appropriate response should be. I still wasn't completely comfortable with them, and she was being so nice to me.

Overtime, she made sure I had more clothes than I could ever imagine owning. Over my time there, she became my fashion icon. She was herself, a very well-dressed woman. She spared no expenses on her clothes, shoes, and hats. Aunt Jodye possessed a great hat collection which was unmatched. If you mentioned Aunt Jodye today, my first memory of her would be how loving she was to me; and how well-dressed she was.

Aunt Jodye was instrumental in raising lawyers, registered nurses, successful realtors, and entrepreneurs. She was the person who built my confidence and allowed me to model for fashion shows next to some of the top local models. Because of her, I could wear clothes from local fashion designers. She also taught me how to wear make-up and how to walk in high heels.

By the time I was 15, she had brought me silk suits, mink coats and anything else that I wanted. She has always been the epitome of all my best experiences. However, back then, she was just a woman who had taken me away from the shelter I had grown to love. The first few weeks in foster care were different than the shelter since it had less structure. I still had my reservations, but it was going well for the most part. I still wasn't too happy about being there, so I would find any and every possible opportunity to get out.

I remember that in the first few months, Aunt Jodye had a busy schedule, but we made it work.

I had to get registered back into public school, but I hated it, especially middle school; the kids were so mean. Eventually, I was sent back to the school I was in before I was removed from my mom's house. I didn't really want to go back there. That school was the worst because the kids were not particularly nice. The boys picked on me because I was a dark-skinned girl, and back in my day, society had accepted light-skinned girls as prettier and smarter. While the boys were bad, the girls were plain bullies. They had no reason to dislike me, but they did anyway. I would often compare myself and wonder how some of their lives would turn out. Now as an adult, I am proud to say I landed on top!

I never bullied other children; I thought that kids should get along, but when I moved to New York in the 80s, bullying was like a recreational activity that people seemed to indulge in just for the sake of it. I never really encountered bullying in the South. Now I see that violence in schools and among children is on the rise today, and it has a lot to do with a child's life at home. Children need to be shown the basic fundamentals of nurturing and understanding. When there is lack in these areas, it can result in many problems such as feelings of loss, pain, and emptiness. I can't imagine anyone taking pleasure in hurting others, but I came to understand that bullies hurt others because they are hurting themselves. Bullies don't realize that their actions hold no rewards in life, and it doesn't get you into the best college, nor does it make you a favorite among your peers. Most of the time, bullies aren't even successful; they just end up as some of the less fortunate individuals of society. This is what I have to say about bullying: "The Bully Always Finishes Last."

I believe that, from the time you're born until you're 18, your home, family, friends, school, and social life should be filled with positive experiences. However, for me and many other kids, this was not the case. During the first week of school, I was terrified, especially with the memories of the last time I attended. My anxiety level was at an all-time high. The teacher in middle school seemed to not care at all and didn't have any control over the students.

I remember how I went to school one day, and during the first class, one of the boys in my class started flirting with me. Another girl got jealous, and we exchanged words. I am sure they were words a child shouldn't use. The teacher yelled, "Stop it! Settle down now!" That day, when class was over, I started walking to second period.

I looked at the door in front of me with the exit sign above it. In an instant, I did just that: I exited the school and walked to my mom's house. I knocked on her door. I don't know what I expected, but I know her reaction wasn't it. As soon as she opened the door, she said, "Why are you here this time of the morning?" I replied, "I left school, I am tired of those kids, the teachers don't care, and I can't take it."

Mom just looked at me for a while and then said, "You can't stay here, you need to go home." Mom knew where my foster home was, so she put on her shoes and coat and walked me home. We walked the distance, and we both were quiet, but eventually, mom broke the silence.

"Natasha, you know I love you, right?"

"Yes, Mom." I replied. In that instance she turned to me and said, "You have to be good, Natasha. I can't help you anymore."

There was something in her voice; I knew she felt as defeated as I did. At that moment, my heart was crushed. It was like someone had sat on my chest and was working to rip my heart out of my body. I fought the tears in my eyes and focused on the road. As we approached the porch, mom again said, "I love you." This time, however, I didn't say it back. I knew I loved her, but I was speechless. I guess hearing my mom say that she could not help me anymore felt as if she would never do anything for me ever again.

As I grew up, I learned what mom meant was that any contact with me had to be approved through the foster care agency and the court system. Yes, as a 'Ward of the Court,' the parents lose their rights to legally make decisions for or on your behalf. I guess you're thinking I really created a mess. I thought that too, back then.

Mom and I walked into the house, and she said hello to Aunt Jodye. Throughout that time, Aunt Jodye kept looking at me with her eyebrows raised. Her questioning look was constantly in front of me, and I couldn't hide away. Aunt Jodye asked, "Why did you leave school?"

I answered, "I don't like the kids, the teachers, or the school."

I didn't realize how much I hated it until I told her with a note of defiance in my voice. I often thought that school would be fun, but it hadn't been fun in a while. Mom and Aunt Jodye talked for a while. They talked far longer than I thought they would. I went into my room and left them. Aunt Jodye then called me from my room to say goodbye to mom.

As we said goodbye, mom gently said, "Be good for Aunt Jodye and go to school." I could only nod at her. Oddly enough, the energy in the room was light and positive as mom left. I watched as she walked out the door and closed it behind her. I stood there for a while, then I felt Aunt Jodye's hand on my shoulder as she led me to the kitchen.

I sat down, and Aunt Jodye and I began talking about school. We talked about the importance of school and that she would call Ms. Mary Alice. She then asked me if I was okay with her doing that. All I knew was that I was not going back to school, and even if I were, it wouldn't be that school for sure. I stayed home the next few weeks, and during that time, I would go out with Aunt Jodye until I started being homeschooled.

It turned out; that I was a straight A student! Ms. Fox, my tutor, would come weekly. Often, she would jokingly ask me if someone was doing my schoolwork for me. Each time, my reply would be,

"Not at all."

CHAPTER 7

A NEW FAMILY

A few months had passed while in foster care. I started to trust and love Aunt Jodye. She was supportive of anything concerning me, she treated me as her own child, she continued to be part of my relationship with my mother. Aunt Jodye in such a short time had begun exposing me to the nicer things in life, fine dining, going to galas and other events. When I came to her with my school problems, she worked with the school district and caseworkers to have me homeschooled and when I was ready she assisted with getting me into a great school. Eventually, I ended up adjusting well in my new school. In foster care, I was also blessed to have a great gentleman in my life a psychiatrist, by the name of Dr. Joe Bell. He was ordered by the court to oversee my psychiatric care.

Even though I wasn't all that grateful to him when I was younger, I grew up to see his worth. Over the years, he was the man that allowed me the opportunity to express how I felt about being separated from my mother, and other issues with-out passing any judgement. He was the one who helped me express how I felt about living in a shelter and how I was coping with living in a foster home. He helped me through the most difficult moments of my life. I remember how heated the counseling sessions with mom used to be. As a child dealing with so much trauma, I would go into those sessions mad at my mom. I resented her for being mentally ill, for the judge taking me, and for her beatings. I was angry with her, and I would yell at her. Then, in some sessions, I simply wouldn't speak to her. I blamed her for putting me through so much at such an early age.

Aunt Jodye would be in the sessions along with Dr. Bell, and they functioned as mediators. Regardless of everything, mom and I would cry in every session. I would yell and be very uncaring of mom's emotions, hell, I was trying to sort out my own. All I could think about at that time was how no one else in the room lived in foster care but me, and that was why no one really could relate with me or understand my pain.

It was through this period that Aunt Jodye managed to develop a great relationship with my mother and came to understand and love her just as she did me. The more she got to know my mom, the more she realized how she needed to be nurtured as well. Because of this, they spoke daily. Even on days when I didn't speak to mom, I knew what was going on in her life because she would talk to Aunt Jodye about it. Mom even started coming over weekly to help Aunt Jodye clean. How I would clean in comparison to my mom would seem like I did nothing or did not know what I was doing. Now, all Aunt Jodye's friends would hire mom to clean for them. They enjoyed her company and conversation as well. I had to admit, mom's smile was infectious. She loved to laugh, and others reciprocated that to her.

Aunt Jodye wanted to see everyone happy. She was instrumental in connecting family members together. She had compassion for others, and she believed in families being united. She was the definition of a perfect woman, and I never once doubted it. She had dedicated her life to helping family members, community members, and strangers as well. She made sure they all had a place to go to. I think when God made her, he knew the world had many people who would need her. Overall, I was in a wonderful place. However, mom and I still had the regular court-appointed family sessions. I was never a fan of those. Every time we discussed the past, our feelings, how we got there, and every other depressing detail that separated me from mom, just made me angry all over again.

As a teenager, you're trying to block bad thoughts and feelings. That is why, at that time, therapy was something I hated. I never realized just how much it was helping me until I grew older and became wiser. It was then that I learned how therapy provided me with the tools to deal with things that made me depressed or uncomfortable.

I do believe that therapy paid off at one point because mom, Aunt Jodye, and I finally got on the same page. Aunt Jodye, Mom, and I had spoken privately, and we made the joint decision that I would remain in foster care with Aunt Jodye. We told the judge in my next court appointment, and he approved the request. This was great for everyone. Everything was under control after that. Mom had accepted Aunt Jodye as being important for both of us, and I had accepted that I needed Aunt Jodye as well as my mom. This marked the point where the bond between me and Aunt Jodye became unbreakable. I could not see myself leaving her. This was not because my mom had not improved in her parenting skills, but instead, we knew that Aunt Jodye was the glue that would keep mom and I together peacefully and help mend old wounds.

Don't get me wrong, mom and I still had moments where we were not communicating effectively. Mom had times when she resented my relationship with Aunt Jodye. However, good ole "Jodye B," which we sometimes referred to Aunt Jodye as, had become an expert for giving us relationship advice. Aunt Jodye knew how to bring calm waters to a storm.

Sometimes, things with mom could spin out of control. It was never intentional, but I just felt like mom had moments when reality just escaped her. We could always tell when mom was getting sick. She wouldn't sleep for days. This is how we knew she was having one of her manic episodes. She would talk at a faster pace than usual, and she would have episodes of paranoia and hallucinations.

While I always held a deep love for my mother, I began to love her even more as I got older. I felt so sad for her. She really didn't deserve this illness. I heard rumors that mental illness ran in our family, but other than my mother, I never saw any symptoms in anyone else. My biological aunt was always there for my mother. Mom went through a lot of changes while I was in foster care, and while some were great, others weren't as good. She moved to a new apartment, committed herself to living a life of religion and faith and remained in a great relationship with her current boyfriend.

When my aunt passed, Aunt Jodye and I thought my mom would have a mental breakdown. We were all terrified about the effect it would have on her. But while mom had episodes every now and then, she normally just remained strong. We all knew how difficult this phase would be for her, and that is when Aunt Jodye stepped up more. Aunt Jodye just knew what my mom needed. I know, without a doubt, that mom and I were blessed when Aunt Jodye allowed us to be a part of her life.

The process might have been long and not without trial and error. However, I ended up in the best foster care home for me; with the best foster mother. I had finally found a place I could call home. Every Sunday, Aunt Jodye and I would go to church. On Wednesday when I had no school or other obligation. I would go with Aunt to the church food pantry.

Aunt Jodye and a group of her close friends started and operated a food pantry to provide food for the elderly and anyone else who needed it. Mom would often come over on Wednesdays to help Aunt Jodye with the church food pantry. They would give food and household items as well as cook a hot meal for the seniors. This is where I first understood the concept of truly giving back to those less fortunate.

I think that as a foster child, it was extremely easy to become selfish, mainly because you're just trying to survive. However, helping others during your own trials and tribulations taught me how to share while allowing me to appreciate the trivial things. I believe that helping others also allowed me to see that there are other people going through problems as well and that it wasn't just me. It was that moment in life that I made up my mind to be a person of service. Now that I am older, I encourage every foster child to help others. Helping the elderly serves as a valuable experience. It allows you to spend time with someone who expects nothing in return except an enjoyable conversation. They are often appreciative of spending time with you and sharing their words of wisdom.

They are the ones with much more experience to share! They have knowledge to educate, inspire and motivate other individuals. Speaking from my personal experience, the best pieces of advice I've ever received came from the elderly. The funniest thing I can remember, when I was in my 20's on a journey to find my way, I took a part-time job working as a Food Pantry Coordinator. I became more like Aunt Jodye than I'd realized!

Over time, I realized how much I enjoyed having a foster mother who treated me as if I was her own child. I enjoyed Aunt Jodye's teachings. My foster family became like my biological family. We fought, we argued, and we loved. We celebrated major holidays like Thanksgiving. Aunt Jodye was an outstanding cook. We had Thanksgiving dinner every year and invited at least 20 or more people to the feast. We would all eat so much food that some of us would end up needing naps.

While Thanksgiving was great, Christmas was the actual holiday which held a completely different level of fun. We always had a White Christmas tree. Since Aunt Jodye was used to doing everything to perfection, she made sure our holidays were perfect as well. Our tree touched the ceiling, and it had lots of gifts under it. Christmas time felt surreal! We made sure that every member of the family got exactly what they wanted.

Every year, Aunt Jodye and I oversaw buying gifts, and she spared no expense. We made sure we had the best celebrations for every holiday and events which were important to all family members. I would say that, out of all the members of my foster family, I was the closest to Aunt Jodye's son, her nephew, and two of her nieces, both of whom were her godchildren. They made me feel special, and I shared a lot of happy moments with them.

I always appreciated Aunt Jodye's son. By the time I had entered foster care, he shared his mom's love with dozens of children. He truly did become my older brothers.

Her nephew was one of the five children that Aunt Jodye took in at the beginning when she first became a foster mother. I often heard he was Aunt Jodye's favorite and that she spoiled him when he was a child. She did the same to me, which is why we got along. Her nieces were my best friends. We acted more like sisters. We did everything together!

I have one cousin who I consider my sister, best friend, and her name is Towana, and we are still close. We lost track of each other, but while I was in foster care, we found each other again. Aunt Jodye accepted Towana, and she became an extension of my foster family.

Towana and I are close even though she was not placed in foster care, she had taken care of herself since she was fifteen. The two of us have had several difficult moments, but I can say now that she has been my rock for more than thirty years.

Aunt Jodye had a niece, CC, who came along when I was older. Aunt Jodye went and picked her up from a foster home. She became my baby and my goddaughter legally. I loved her and still love her today. If there's one thing I know, it is that I would never change any one of my foster family members. They were and remain important and indispensable parts of my life.

When you're a foster child, sometimes you believe that you have been dealt a wrong hand. You become very suspicious of people's intentions. You start to think that no one really cares about you, even if they do care. I may not have known it then, but I learned that most of the case workers, therapists, and support service workers are genuinely committed to helping others. If adults find it difficult to trust, then know that it's twice as hard for children. Therefore, it's important that children are loved, nurtured, and given the tools that allow them to understand their emotions and deal with them in a productive and self-preserving way. A foster parent's love should have no boundaries. It should be unconditional even if the child being cared for is being disrespectful and unreceptive.

While I do feel that my foster care experience was probably better than other foster children, it is important to note that having Aunt Jodye as a great foster mother and her stability of didn't get rid of my pain. However, it did do was help me cope. Aunt Jodye always said that she understood my anger, but that if I respected her and was receptive of her love, she would always be there for me—she meant just that. Even today, I often think of the unbreakable bond that Aunt Jodye and I had.

It often made others jealous, even my mom. I remember one day, Aunt Jodye's biological aunt who had Alzheimer's said to us, *"Jodye, I remember when you gave birth to her. She's still running her mouth, but she is pretty as ever."* Aunt Jodye and I chuckled, and neither of us corrected her because I was not Aunt Jodye's biological child. But the overwhelming love she poured into me made everyone feel as if she was my biological mother. There was not a time throughout the years that I needed Aunt Jodye, and she was not there. In a way, the experience was necessary because it was that which shaped my purpose in life.

Despite the horror stories, I would say that being in foster care was a necessary surprise. I still hear stories and read about unfortunate foster care experiences and my heart goes out to any foster child who does not have an Aunt Jodye in their life. I wouldn't say that my foster home was perfect. As I said earlier, Aunt Jodye helped a lot of individuals, unofficially making our foster home: a shelter, a drug rehab center, and a daycare.

While the state had guidelines, Aunt Jodye helped us all at the same time. If you needed help, she would be more than willing to accept the responsibility. While I might not have realized it then, I now admit that foster care was the best choice for me. I would not have the career that I have, and I would never have found my purpose, that is, to care for others—if not for my time in my foster home. My experience in foster care taught me what genuine love and care looks like.

I believe that it's people like Aunt Jodye who truly make the foster care system a success. I also believe that laws should be put in place, and stronger checks and balances be applied, to ensure that great foster parents are provided, and the bad ones are weeded out to give every child a loving home as they truly deserve.

CHAPTER 8

FOSTERING RELATIONSHIPS

Aunt Jodye was a great lady. She was a crucial part of my life when it came to developing many great relationships. She was the woman who taught me how to forgive and move forward. I often wondered where Aunt Jodye, at 60 years of age, found the continual energy to spend her life helping others, build and mend broken relationships.

It was this aspect that allowed me to mend all the flaws and build a decent relationship with my mother. I recall moments when I was disrespectful to my mother primarily because I was upset that she was forced to place me in foster care. However, whenever Aunt Jodye heard it, she immediately said, "That is your mother, you cannot disrespect her in front of me." I'm not going to lie; I would then get upset with Aunt Jodye mainly because I felt like she was taking my mom's side over mines and it didn't seem fair. I felt like Aunt Jodye was my foster mother, not my mom, so she should never take anyone's side other than mine. It was only when I got older that

I realized that Aunt Jodye was not taking sides at all. She was just correcting inappropriate behavior. I now realize her true worth and undoubtedly believe that if all the children, especially those in the foster care system, had an Aunt Jodye, then the probability of success in their life would be great.

Though things weren't always perfect, I can still look back and appreciate Aunt Jodye telling me when I was wrong and when I was right. She took great care of me and worked off the guiding principle that relationships are meaningful in both the mental and physical forms. Believing that children should be mentally comforted, Aunt Jodye always made me feel better, even in the worst of situations. She was the one woman whom I could rely on after a distressing day and who would come over and give me warm hugs.

She really changed my life and gave me a prominent relationship other than the one I developed with my mother. My relationship with my foster mother was the one that has truly been the most important for me. No one made more of an impact on me than Aunt Jodye B. Holmes. It still is a mystery to me how her biological son was able to share his mom with so many people from an early age. It is no doubt that he's her only biological child, but he was never the only child in the home. It really takes a strong human being to share their mother, and Aunt Jodye had given that strength to her son.

Aunt Jodye had a way about her that would completely transform you for sure. For me, she managed to instill the value of life. She showed me how to care for others and helped me become who I am, and today, I am a loving, caring, goal-driven and determined person all because of her. I must admit that even regardless of that, I am not without fault. I am apologetic to those along my journey that I caused pain to, was disrespectful to, and offended when I was hurting.

Aunt Jodye also introduced me to many of my childhood role models. I remember a local African American activist, prison reform advocate, and the founder of the Center for Law and Justice, Dr. G. In my time, we could find the activists on our local TV channel fighting for many people's rights. The wonderful thing about Dr. G. is that she and Aunt Jodye were friends.

Aunt Jodye helped so many people, even individuals with a criminal history, and she also worked as a paralegal at the local Legal Aid Society. That was when she and Dr. G. had become friends. I had come to realize that the best thing about Dr. G. was that she did not back down. She was from an era where racial equality was not balanced, and a lot of her work was centered around this issue. However, there was one thing which I knew for sure, and that was how fearless Dr. G. was. It was this that made her my role model.

I can admit that even through all my difficulties, I still cherish all the experiences I had as a melanated girl who grew up in urban America. The wonderful thing about our culture is that it provides experiences early on in life, which prepares you for life's challenges. Most of my memories from foster care are about how Aunt Jodye would take in several women that were addicted to drugs. I watched some of them go through withdrawals, abuse, and family abandonment, but what I could see was how most of those women were simply great people with addiction problems. There isn't one day that I don't think about those women.

Out of all the women that shared my foster home, there was one who was my favorite. Her name was Alene. She was such a sweet person to Aunt Jodye and me. She went in and out of our life, but as Aunt Jodye got older and sick, she helped care for her. She took care of Aunt Jodye like she was her own mother. It was this that truly made me admire her. Even when she was struggling with her own demons, she still took care of my aunt.

Alene always said that she loved Aunt Jodye and me because when others turned their backs on her, we did not. Aunt Jodye and I asked no questions, we just showed others love and compassion. Aunt Jodye raised me well. As I became comfortable in my role, I became the second in charge, especially as Aunt Jodye got older. When she was unable to care for even herself, it was up to me to raise the younger foster children and cousins.

I modeled a lot of Aunt Jodye's behavior, caring for the children in our house just as she did and in some situations, my mannerisms took an uncanny resemblance to hers. I knew what to do when needed just as she had taught me. I know for sure she impacted my life. Without her, my life would be entirely different.

She was a necessity. It is because of her that I strive to help others. She taught me how important it was to share and not be selfish.

Though a lot of my strength is attributed to Aunt Jodye's influential characteristics, I can definitely say that I also drew strength from my mother. I often think about how strong my mom was to have mental illness, and to go through every terrible thing that has ever happened to her, and not to give up on life. It is that strength that I aspire to have. I have often heard from people who suffer through the same mental illness and how they talk about their incessant need to give up. However, in my mom's case, she had never felt the need to simply let go. Mom just dealt with the hand that the Spiritual Father gave her, and now that I look at it, all I can say is, *wow*. In recognizing her strength, as I got older, my mom became my role model. My mom was not only strong but had an unwavering love for me.

I have great admiration for strong women and aspire to be one myself. Today, I look for key role models and mentors amongst women who face numerous challenges daily. Despite our obstacles, we are here in the 21st century, becoming self- made millionaires, business moguls, top executives in major companies, and so much more. We, as women, have managed to find our voice, and we decided that if men could become wealthy and famous, then why can't we? As we see the growing record of women-owned businesses and even higher numbers of minority-owned businesses, it gives me hope.

I watched Aunt Jodye over the years, as she operated a local food pantry, a program for senior citizens and other ventures. Through that, I knew that I had to grow and do remarkable things. At the forefront of anything, I do it to improve someone else's quality of life. I choose to live my life as a servant, one who unselfishly puts others first and helps people in need. In the society we live in today, we see that there is a growing need for mentors and role models.

They encourage us when needed, while also teaching us important lessons and motivating us to be the best person we can be. They model behaviors that we duplicate in our own actions and lives. It is particularly important that we find role models, mentors, and individuals that motivate us and teach us how to bring out the best part of us. These are the people we can find anywhere, schools, churches, neighborhood communities, workplaces and even home. We must identify what we want in a role model and mentor, then seek individuals with those qualities. This gives us the privilege to connect with like-minded people.

If I did not have Aunt Jodye as a role model or even my mother, then quite frankly, I would not know how to carry myself as a lady. While I know that they were not perfect, they were two different people who contributed to raising one young girl. What I know for sure is that healthy relationships and role models are important in the development of children's lives. They provide a balance of nurture and appreciation. They teach them directions on what to do and not to do. I can't help but ask how foster parents and agencies that are trusted to care for children are unable to understand the additional basic needs of children outside of food, water, clothing, and shelter. We need to encourage awareness of such matters if we are to create a healthy society.

All children need nurturing from adults in their lives. This includes the on-going feeling of being cared for, encouraged, and feeling safe. These attributes are essential during a child's growing and developing stages. I often wonder how a parent could intentionally neglect to give a child these vital life necessities. After all, coming into the world was not a choice that the child made. It's up to the parents to protect and provide regardless of economic status or personal situations. Encouragement and contributing to mental growth and emotional safety is free and should be given freely as well.

Whether it's a case of a foster or biological child, we must encourage children to express themselves. I grew up in the 'Yes' and 'No' era. We only answered when we were spoken to. And in the world today, children are vulnerable in communities plagued with poverty, mental illness, and other problems. The most important thing we should offer to our children is love, healthy relationships, and positive role models or mentors. That is how we build a community of healthy, nurturing, and strong individuals.

CHAPTER 9

AN ENTREPRENUER WAS BORN

I continued my stay in foster care while working on my relationship with my mom. During that time, I attended high school, worked a part-time job, and made time to hang out with friends. Young adulthood didn't treat me as badly as I thought it would. I began early in life, figuring out how I could make money. All my struggles and the places I lived taught me, from an incredibly young age, just how necessary money was.

In foster care, although I had Aunt Jodye, I knew that I would have to learn to be financially independent. I wasn't from a wealthy family background, and I would have no one to support me. That's why, at the mere age of 14, I started attending after school programs that paid stipends for attending. I still remember how it felt getting my first stipend check. It wasn't as much as I would've liked, but it was a step toward progress. I would get paid about $75 every two weeks, and it felt great! I felt self-sufficient. All the incidents from my childhood about money kept coming back to me. I felt like an adult, and like I was doing something worthwhile.

As I grew older, I realized that the money I was making simply wasn't enough. It wasn't greed, but a passion for success. I wanted more money, so I took a job at the local library, stacking books on the shelves. This job paid about one hundred and fifty dollars every two weeks. I thought I was taking one step up, much like George Jefferson from the show *The Jeffersons*. I started feeling that the more money I made, the more money I wanted. It was something that struck me at a young age. I was eager to excel and loved to work. It was just one of those things that my childhood and living with Aunt Jodye taught me. If I wanted anything, I had to work for it.

I was able to buy things without asking Aunt Jodye, waiting on my monthly foster care stipend, or the Social Security check, which I received monthly from my mother because of her disability. I was focused on my studies, but even more focused on finding ways on how I could earn more. I would call it motivation. I continued school, but after school, I worked. Eventually, I realized that my hunger for money was increasing.

When I was 17, I recall seeing a job classified in the Sunday Newspapers, which read something like *'Local Hospital Looking for Patient Care Technician.'* I was over the moon. It required no experience, paid training, and the instructions were to come to the local hospital to apply. I got out of bed the next day and rushed to get dressed.

I skipped school, took the bus to complete the job application, and got a call shortly thereafter for an interview. This was officially going to be my first real job. Aunt Jodye helped me practice. She guided me on the dos and don'ts of how I should sit and speak. By the end, I was confident.

I was beyond excited. I had no experience working in a hospital or the healthcare field. I walked into the hospital and went to the Human Resources office as instructed. Everything that I learned was circulating in my head. I took a deep breath to compose myself. The receptionist greeted me and provided some additional forms to complete before asking me to take a seat. After waiting a short while, a woman with a lab coat approached me. Her brunette hair reached her shoulders; she had the kindest eyes. I was immediately at ease. She introduced herself as Ms. Kathy, the head nurse. She was responsible for hiring for the new Geriatric Unit being developed.

She began asking several different questions and liked each of my replies. After speaking with her for a few minutes, she stood up and led me to the door. I was a little heartbroken because I thought I had been rejected after a fantastic interview. However, Ms. Kathy followed me out and told me she was taking me to the new department location. My face lit up again, and she smiled.

After leaving the human resource office, Ms. Kathy and I took the elevator to tour the unit that she was hiring for. It was cold, ominous, and under construction in certain areas. I looked around taken in every detail. It was all too familiar a place since I had witnessed my grandmother pass. There were people who wore white coats, and others in colored uniforms. They moved all around the area, absorbed in their work. I felt almost invisible. At one point, some of the elderly patients were sitting on the recliners with restraints and white sheets on them. Some were yelling. I couldn't stop looking at them. They looked like they were in so much pain.

I tried to ignore their painful stares and just smiled and spoke to them as I walked by. It really made me miss my grandmother. Here I was, looking at the last stages of a person's life. This is what happens as a person gets older. It hit me then how much I missed my own family, but I focused my energy on Ms. Kathy as she continued introducing me to the patients and the staff.

As we walked, one of the nurses came up to her. Her name was Ms. Beverly. She was a melanated, so it was nice to meet someone with the same skin complexion as me who was vital to the lives of others. It was very impressive. At the end of the tour, Ms. Kathy told me that she would inform Human Resources to go through with the hiring process and that if I met all the requirements, she would hire me.

I left feeling great. I was confident that I would get the job. A few days later, after they reviewed my credentials, I was told I met all the requirements and was hired. The only catch was that I was still in school, and training would be for one week during school hours. I didn't let that trouble me. I was adamant about getting a position, and I took the week off from school and attended training. Something in me said, *"You have to take this job."* I listened to the voice, and it all paid off. I don't condone missing school, and neither did Aunt Jodye, but it was for a noble cause. I did it to help people in need, and that made me feel like I was doing something worthy. It was a great learning opportunity as well. I met so many patients' families who told me exceptional stories which kept me encouraged.

I learned the true meaning of helping and the power of healing. Some of my patients would leave, some would return, and some would never go home. I can honestly say that I never had a patient that did not appreciate the work I did. Even on their most challenging days, they attempted to display grace.

I was attached to some patients more than others. One who comes to mind was named Rosemary, a sweet little Italian lady. She was so funny, and boy, could she curse! I admired her determination, and her family was the true definition of a family. I watched her children visit her daily, sometimes even twice a day. They would always bring food with them, sometimes her lunch and dinner. They celebrated holidays with her, all of them, including her grandkids. It was really sweet.

I worked as a Patient Care Technician for a year. Then, I was promoted to a position as a Unit Secretary. I really enjoyed both jobs. It allowed me to have contact with patients and their family members. I guess, in some ways, working in the hospital was therapeutic for me. I enjoyed helping others, and perhaps that was something I had learned from Aunt Jodye; it felt second nature to me.

Even in the most challenging times, we all need someone to help us. Over the years, I have watched people go in and out of my life…some days we were speaking, then some days we were not. However, the thing that I always knew was that I could depend on my foster mother and my mother to love me unconditionally.

My mother was a wonderful woman. I often wondered how she could spend her entire life being so fascinated and in love with me. Even when I was not the best child, she still managed to remain the best mother that she knew how to be. As I got older, my appreciation for her only increased. What I know for sure is that a child needs to know that someone cares. The love you receive as a child impact who you grow up to become. The feeling of loneliness or the lack of love tends to manifest in ways that can somehow become dangerous to the child or others that the child encounters.

We, as adults, must provide an overwhelming amount of love, care, and concern in the lives of the children. This is what makes them successful business owners, entrepreneurs, and so forth. For me, my mother and Aunt Jodye's unconditional support was what created that passion in me to help people. The struggles of my past made me empathetic and desperate to succeed. My upbringing helped feed my hunger for success and gave me a drive for entrepreneurship.

I recall starting a necktie business after seeing an ad in a local magazine. It read, "Wholesale Neck Ties," and I ended up ordering 50 of them. I sold those ties to our neighbors, church members, to Aunt Jodye's insurance agent, and anyone else who would buy them. In the end, I was left with no ties and $1,200. That drove me to the realization that I could do so much more. That, along with the paycheck from the hospital, left me with more money than I had imagined.

I learned some valuable lessons working at such an early age. As a child entrepreneur, my first lesson was that not everyone would see my vision. My vision was simply that—my vision. When I'd first told my friends about the neckties, they thought that it was the craziest idea ever. However, Aunt Jodye and my cousins continued to support my hard work. What I said to myself then, and what I say to everyone now, is that you must be confident in yourself to get the job done. The point to note is that this goes for either an employee or entrepreneur: *Believe in yourself.*

The next business I pursued was babysitting. I decided that I was going to start an at-home daycare approved through the local social service agency. As always, Aunt Jodye was on board with the support. Hell, on some days, she even helped me care for the children. I loved babysitting.

Spending time with babies and young children always took my stress away. It felt extremely rewarding. Over the years, I kept track of their progress. Only recently, I found out that one of the babies I babysat is now a music entrepreneur and another is a fashion designer. I could not be prouder of these young entrepreneurs.

While babysitting, I began to shop, party, and not save any money. One day, two of my kid's parents decided that they were moving out of the state. I knew that meant my money was moving out of the state as well…I had not saved one dime.

That's when I learned just how important it was to budget and save. Businesses are always changing, and they're risky. Your finances can change at any time, and if you're not prepared, it could cause you financial hardship. I recommend all business owners have an accountant, but if you can't afford one, then it's best to get a bookkeeper. Either way, it's necessary to have your finances straight.

I also recommend children to embrace classes in school, such as math, reading, and writing. These are the fundamentals, and if they don't have these three skills, then they end up at the mercy of others. It's even more critical if you have your own business. It helps you protect the business from the dangers of mismanagement.

I recall another mistake I made early in business ventures. I did not keep the greatest business records.

There are so many entrepreneurs, small business owners, and side hustlers nowadays; everyone is their own boss. However, that does not mean that they are good or should even be in business for themselves. To be honest, some are con artists simply looking for money, power and they can care less about respect, dignity, or others. Unfortunately, today with the new age entrepreneurs, most don't have the business system or structure in place to sustain or grow their business. I once saw a social media post, and it said something like, "How can you trust someone who failed math class and dropped out of high school to do your taxes?"

I believe in second chances, but I advise everyone to be careful who you work with. Not everyone can be trusted, and nor are they qualified to conduct business. I had the fantastic opportunity to watch Aunt Jodye, Dr. G., Ms. Kathy, and so many others as I was on my career and entrepreneurial journey. I picked up lessons and skills from each of these women and others. I learned self-discipline as well as self-worth.

Regardless of the positions they reached, I saw how each of these women stayed true to who they were. They all came from different walks of life, but the one thing they all had in common was that they were confident in themselves. Confidence is the greatest strength that one could have. You should have the unwavering ability to trust yourself, as well as the strength to carry on when times are rough. Times will get rough, especially as an entrepreneur. It's vital that you understand that and do not lose faith. I have had many difficulties in my life, but I always knew that God would see me through. Even in my darkest hours, I saw a light at the end of the tunnel.

Often, people tell me how strong I am, and I can't help but thank my mother for that strength. She and I had to be strong when the courts decided to separate our mother-daughter bond. No matter what I did or did not like about her, she was my biological mother. She was the first woman to love me unconditionally.

My strength was tested, and I always managed to come back stronger. I believe that all of us can be entrepreneurs. It's just that some choose to bring it out, and others prefer a different path to gain financial stability.

I will say that, regardless of the path you choose, your skills will determine your success. Remember, success is earned rather than given, and maintained rather than borrowed. I worked in the hospital for about two years. There was a time when a patient arrived, and I had to work on his admission chart. I entered his room to introduce myself and placed his name tag on his door and above his bed. I always enjoyed meeting new patients.

Their stories always kept me interested. Since I worked on the geriatric floor, there was a lot of history to be learned. Patients from diverse backgrounds shared different life experiences. When I went to see a new patient. I approached the room divider to say hello. Instead, I was greeted by a lady who immediately said, "I am his caretaker, and he does not talk."

I was taken aback by her quick delivery of words. I still proceeded to say hello to him even when I knew he would not reply. I discovered that he was an individual with 'special needs,' a great gift from above. I made it a point to keep daily checks on him. I would say hello and ask him if he was okay. There were occasions when his caretaker would not show up, and the hospital staff would be busy. I would be required to sit with him and feed him. I enjoyed those moments; watching him with all his innocence would always bring a new meaning to life.

One day I went in, and his caretaker was there. We ended up striking a conversation, which turned out to be quite enlightening. I learned about the agency where he resided, why he was there, and other details. That conversation sparked something inside of me; it was then that I realized the direction my career would take. I researched, and after two and a half years, I left working in the hospital to go work in the Community and Human Service Field. I worked in a few various aspects of this field. I worked with homeless individuals in transitional homes and seniors in an adult living facility. However, the area where I could say my strengths were utilized most was working with individuals with special needs.

These were the people who brought me the most happiness. I went into this field willing and wanting to learn, and luckily, I was able to move up the ladder quickly. I went from being a low-level employee to a mid-level supervisor, all in two years. I enjoyed working there so much that I obtained my degree in Community and Human Service Management. I often said that I could not sing, act, or do any of those wonderful things. However, I have the best career that has allowed me to change other people's lives and have influence.

I know that God knew who and what I would be before I was born. He chose the steps I would take, even when they were difficult. In the end, he carried me to my destination. I could go on about the many lessons I've learned as an individual and as an entrepreneur, but I won't. What I will say is being a decent person and great entrepreneur comes with responsibilities. These responsibilities include:

1. Your willingness to learn – You never truly know everything, but you can learn from mentors, take classes, or look at others doing the same business as you. You should never assume you're the smartest in the room.

2. Your willingness to identify your strengths and weaknesses – Not everyone is perfect, we all have great things that make us who we are, and we all have things on which we can improve. Knowing your strengths and weaknesses allows you become a better person; while building and growing a successful business. It helps you identify those areas where you can help and support others.

3. Having the willingness to share ideas, thoughts, and information – You must not give your complete business information away. However, sharing limited information allows collaboration, which could lead to business growth. It will enable transparency and promote business allies.

4. The ability to hire a talented team – You do not have the answers to every question. That is why it is essential to hire knowledgeable people to help you make your vision come true. The greatest stars and business owners hire great people to help them get to the top, so why not do the same?

5. Build great relationships and friendships with other great entrepreneurs – Entrepreneurs are all chasing their dreams and independence. They can be great soundboards. They give you strength and motivate you in times of need. You can't go wrong with a few loyal business friends. They will only help you to become a greater person.

6. Take care of the customers – When providing products or services, it's crucial to ensure it is done with love. I often come across bad services from businesses, and that results in them losing current and potential customers. When I call customer support, I want to be appreciated for spending my hard-earned dollars. I recommend all entrepreneurs and business owners to take a course in customer service, put in place customer service quality checks. The driving force behind success is the almighty dollar, and if no one is spending their money on your business, then it means that you're leaving behind your dream of financial wealth.

Most individuals want to be great entrepreneurs, but some fail at being a great leader. You need to understand that, just because you have a high ranking, position, your own business, and employees, it does not mean you're a great leader. What I do is I make notes of some of the best quotes and operate based on what they say. Here's a couple of my favorite quotes by Robin S. Sharma:

"Victims recite problems. Leaders present solutions."

-and-

"There's a much deeper power than titled power."

There is also this quote which is most influential in my leadership style:

"The true test of a man's character is what he does when no one is watching."—*John Wooden*

A great leader is not a victim. In my entrepreneurial journey, I did not expect any handouts and I didn't want anything for free. I have come across individuals who want to be entrepreneurs, but they want sympathy. From such people, I'd like to ask, "How can you lead others if you can't resolve your own problems?"

A leader should aim to solve problems instead of creating them. It's also important to know that a title means absolutely nothing if you don't have the characteristics, skills, and knowledge that leaders need to possess. If you don't have those skills, then you will fail in the leadership department.

A good leader is honest, loyal, and committed, even when no one is watching. They have outstanding moral and ethical values. No one wants to work for a disloyal, dishonest, and uncommitted person. If you are this way, how long do you think your entrepreneurial journey will last? A great leader naturally leads others on a progressive journey, and they don't intentionally sabotage themselves or those that look up to them. They also have loyal followers, despite their title, money, or power. Their followers and employees trust in their vision because of their exceptional ability to lead.

CHAPTER 10

A CHIILD'S ACTION PLAN

Through my journey in foster care, there's a lot that I have learned. I want to emphasize how important it is to have an action plan while in foster care. Unfortunately, not every foster parent will be an Aunt Jodye, a caring and loving woman who fulfills all the child's needs.

In today's society, you will find some foster parents that are emotionally, verbally, and physically abusive, and others that will only be in it for money. This is the primary reason you must start thinking about your life inside foster care, regardless of whether you return to your biological parents, or age out of foster care. Your journey from there will only be shaped by your lessons and preparation.

You must have certain tools to navigate inside and outside of the foster home and foster care system. You must access the support and resources available, and this will allow you to leave foster care inspired, motivated, and with as much knowledge as possible to live and work productively in society. There are certain things that I believe are helpful when working on your action plan. I will list them down now.

1. You must **work on your mental health** issues and complete a self-assessment.

I learned that I attained mental peace by mending my relationship with my mother. I did that with Aunt Jodye's help, but even then, I had to do the major portion of the work. So, it's crucial that you utilize any psychiatric or mental health therapy available. I know by now you're probably thinking, "Who wants to see a shrink? There's nothing wrong with me!" You're absolutely right... nothing is wrong with you personally, however the events that led up to foster care and being in foster care were traumatic, life-changing events, so having someone to talk to is a great benefit.

Whether you have good foster parents or not, you need to seek professional help, sort out your feelings and gain professional insight on how to best handle those feelings. Now, I am not saying that this will remove your thoughts or change it entirely, but for me, it offered tools that I could utilize when I felt sad. Yes, I know this may be a lot for a young child, but it's necessary. Since it's such a long process, this needs to begin shortly after being placed in foster care.

2. I have already spoken about fostering necessary relationships. However, you must **develop healthy relationships.**

The intention to have a great relationship with our foster parent(s) is present at the start, but as I said before, that does not always turn out to be the case. I encourage you to look at other opportunities and build relationships outside of your foster home, such as with your social worker, case worker, and medical provider, church official, or members or school personnel. You must realize that the more relationships you build, the better it will be for you. The reason is that you want to create additional opportunities where you can feel safe to share information, especially if things are not great within your foster home.

While we hope that all foster parents have great intentions, that's not always the case. As a foster child, you must report any time you believe you are being abused, neglected, or exploited. If you are unfortunate enough to have ended up in foster care, then you have been through something terrible. That's also why it is unacceptable to continue living in hell in your foster home.

3. You need to **learn how to communicate effectively.**

What I mean by that is that you should not allow anyone to take your voice from you. You must communicate clearly. You need to ensure that your agreements and disagreements are heard and understood. I was very vocal as a child and not always in the most respectful manner, but I said exactly how I felt.

I recall one particular relationship, which made me lose my voice. I temporarily accepted emotional, verbal, and physical abuse that I should not have accepted. I attributed this to my dad being absent in my life. Because of that, I believed in loving someone so much that you accept their faults even when it's not healthy. You need to understand that when you see yourself losing your voice, this is where those healthy relationships are utilized.

You will come across people and situations that will test your ability to communicate effectively throughout your life, but you have to remember to communicate your 'Yes' and your 'No' effectively and seek help right away.

No one has the right to **ABUSE**, **NEGLECT,** or **EXPLOIT** you. Ever. Learn to speak loudly and speak clearly until you are heard. Through my journey, I am now able to speak clearly, voice my opinions and thoughts across in a loud but respectful, polite, and professional manner. I see it all the time on the news, read articles, and know several others who have lost their voice and have become a victim of abuse. I want no one to become a victim, especially a foster child, after reading this book.

4. Daily Life Skills needed to function today are things you need to keep close.

Life skills are necessary to survive, and you need to make sure you know what they are. These skills include your personal hygiene, grooming, dressing, health care maintenance, nutrition, meal planning, preparation skills, transportation skills, housekeeping, safety, and community skills. I am sure there are many others, but these are the ones I find most important when leaving foster care.

For example, proper care of your personal hygiene is necessary because it allows you to be more approachable and presentable. Most people want to live and work with a person that cares about themselves, and this is the number one way to identify that. Always remember, don't hesitate when it comes to hygiene simply because you don't know how to complete personal hygiene and grooming skills. Always ask someone, like your foster parent, caseworker, or teacher. They are there to help you learn and improve in this area.

Equally important is your health. You must learn tips to maintain optimal health. Make sure you get regular medical check-ups, visit the dentist twice a year, go to the eye doctor annually, and drink water throughout the day. The point is that, once you're an adult, these tasks become your sole responsibility, and that's why you need to be more in charge of it. Also, you need to be able to plan and prepare meals and eat foods that are nutritionally good for you.

On top of that, you also need to have transportation skills most of the time when you leave foster care. You need to learn how to utilize public transportation systems like buses, rideshare programs, and trains according to where you live.

You should also have the appropriate safety skills you need to be able to watch for strangers and safely utilize varies modes of transportation. When planning your routes, keep in mind the unsafe neighborhoods.

The point to all this is that, while in foster care, you must start learning and preparing for your adult life. Remember, as foster kids, we are already at a disadvantage at maintaining family relationships, and that's precisely why, regardless of the outcome, as an adult, you must be capable of caring for yourself and ensuring your well-being.

5. After you've addressed your mental health, created a healthy relationship, learned to communicate effectively, and developed your life skills. Now, your next step is to start thinking about your **employment and career goals**.

During my time in foster care, I was presented with the opportunity to watch Aunt Jodye, church leaders, community leaders, and neighbors be of service to others. Under their constant care, I started to know exactly what I would do as an adult. They were my inspiration, and I started the journey of being a caretaker by observing the people around me. It's crucial to decide who and what you will be. The future career path you take eventually defines your purpose. The reason is that, in foster care, you're a ward of the court.

In most cases, the courts do not set aside funds for you to attend college or vocational training, neither is it a requirement for your foster parent to set aside monies for you to pursue your educational endeavors. You may not even have biological family members who are financially stable enough to pay for your education. Therefore, you could be solely responsible for your educational expenses.

I recommend that you start researching and learning what options are available while you're in foster care. whether it's college, vocational career training, or the military, anything of the sort is a great deal. It helps foster children avoid circumstances like being homeless, drug addicts, victims of human trafficking, or find themselves in other unfortunate circumstances.

I recall applying to colleges and getting accepted, but Aunt Jodye didn't push me to go to college right after completing high school. Quite frankly, I could have lived with Aunt Jodye for the rest of her life. In fact, we used to laugh and say, "Aunt Jodye, you did not force me to go to college, and I missed out on the college experience."

Jokingly, she would reply, "This is a college experience. Look how many foster children you've helped me raise! Every one of them successfully went through the "University of 241." We would both chuckle. I didn't mind missing college because I didn't want to leave Aunt Jodye; since she was getting older. I then went on to get my associate and bachelor's degree through our local university.

If you're still undecided about what you want to do with your life, then I would recommend that you research your options and speak with your case manager. Through that, you will be able to see what funding if any is available to a foster child. You can also talk with your school guidance counselors, and they can arrange career and aptitude testing for you as well. This can help you identify what skills and tasks you're good at and what steps you need to take to be successful.

The worst case is that if you're still undecided, but you're still in foster care, you can have resources and support to help and motivate you. It's vital that, as a foster child, you leave foster care knowing precisely what you will do with your life. When the support and resources are gone, it's a little more challenging to navigate on your own. I'm not saying that it's impossible; it can be done, but it is better that you utilize the resources when they are available to you. I want to encourage all foster care children to become Mentees, Interns, or Volunteers because it is through these acts that you can find the motivation to become better. I enjoyed going with Aunt Jodye and volunteering at our church food pantry, along with several other activities she had me go to with her. As a foster child, it was a great way to give back as well as learn from those who were less fortunate than me. I sometimes used to go there to simply listen to the stories, and they were all so inspirational.

The great thing about learning is it's the one thing that can never be taken from you; it can be useful and shared with others throughout your life. I suggest that you find programs of interest with the assistance of your foster parents, caseworkers, and school, which can support your personal and potential career growth. I know that, if I had not had some of the opportunities that foster care presented me with, I would not be who I am today. I say that to all the great foster parents, biological parents, family members, mentors, and advocates. I salute each of you on behalf of every foster child and all children that you positively impacted.

CONCLUSION

There will come a day when you will need to transition from your foster home and into your own living environment. Therefore, it is best to be knowledgeable, prepared, and aware of your next steps. Yes, the big day will come, so as a foster child, you should be thinking in advance about where you will live. Will it be with your friends, or at your own apartment? If it's the latter, then you must identify how you will transition into living in your own space.

I stayed with Aunt Jodye for about another five years after aging out of foster care; she was getting older, and, honestly, she was my best friend. However, that may not be an option for you, which is why you need to start thinking about rent costs, security deposits, and the neighborhood you may want to live in. Research everything associated with housing and do whatever is in your power.

Your decision must be well-planned; you don't want to be homeless or dependent on others for shelter. Remember, we have worked hard to turn this experience into a positive one, and every step you take should be planned out well to ensure the most success possible. Once you reach the big day when it's time to leave foster care, keep in mind that we have become strong. We have been forever changed, inspired by others, and motivated to end this journey.

We began a new journey in our life, so, even though our biological family may not have been the best, or even in our lives, we survived. We survived when life threw us curveballs, and other adults let us down. We gathered the strength to change our lives, and we believed that we were worthy of greatness, so we set out to be a greater person. We beat the odds that were stacked high against us.

This is why I ask every foster child to leave, "Foster Care with A Purpose." Others may know your story, but no one can tell it better than you. In addition, sharing your story can greatly impact the life of another foster child, parent, social worker, human being. Strive to be a part of changing rules and regulations within the foster care system. I know that's exactly what I did, and what I continue to do today!

www.ingramcontent.com/pod-product-compliance
Lightning Source LLC
LaVergne TN
LVHW051104080426

835508LV00019B/2053